COPING WITH LANGUAGE:
TALK YOUR WAY TO SUCCESS

MARY McGANN

Illustrated by
M. Susan Flynn

RICHARDS ROSEN PRESS, INC.

NEW YORK, N.Y. 10010

1-7-82

Published in 1980 by Richards Rosen Press, Inc.
29 East 21st Street, New York, N.Y. 10010

First Edition

Library of Congress Cataloging in Publication Data

McGann, Mary, 1940–
  Coping with language.

  (Coping with series)
    1. Interpersonal communication. 2. Nonverbal
communication (Psychology) 3. Success. I. Title.
BF637.C45M24   158   80–33
ISBN 0–8239–0518–7

Manufactured in the United States of America

About the Author

DR. MARY MCGANN is Associate Professor of Communications at St. Thomas Aquinas College in Sparkill, New York, from which she graduated with honors. Her Master of Arts degree in Speech and Drama was taken at the Catholic University of America in Washington, D.C., and her Doctorate in Education is from Teachers College, Columbia University, in New York City. Her first book, *Enjoying the Arts/Theatre,* was published in 1977. Dr. McGann lectures widely on the sub-  ject of mass communication to civic and business groups.

Contents

Foreword

In the title of this book is the word *talk.* Don't be afraid of it. You have talked, without any help, since you were two minutes old. It is easy to open your mouth and say some words. As an infant you babbled nonsense syllables and jibberish in order to let everyone know how you felt about things. Your system worked. You got *through.* You communicated. Did you ever think that you could talk for fun and profit? It is a proven fact that what words you choose to say, and how you say them, can often mean the difference between the life and death of an idea or the success or failure of a personal goal.

It would help greatly if you could substitute the word *talk* every time you have to *speak,* because talking doesn't bother you half as much as speaking does. If, at school or at work, you find yourself having to give a speech, or just having to "say a few words" on any topic from artichokes to zenias, don't panic. First, relax into talking with yourself about your subject, then talk casually to a handful of friends about it. When you gain enough belief in yourself, you will find that you have simply polished the skill that you were born with. You have used "everyday" talk with "everyday" words.

You may be asking yourself why you have to bother to study the art of talking when you aren't planning to run for public office or become a professional speaker. Have you ever considered that for approximately 70 percent of your waking hours you are actively involved in some kind of communication situation, either talking or listening, ranging anywhere from kaffeeklatsches to formal conversation with your boss? You need, in order to climb the ladder of success, to discuss your ideas at meetings and to express your personal feelings to someone who matters in your life.

As a human person you enjoy many gifts and privileges unshared by the rest of the animate world. If you were to classify the most distinctive of these gifts, the ability to talk, to express yourself through the medium of words, would undoubtedly rank first in the hierarchy of special human talents. Since you do so much talking every day of your life, why not shape it into an art form? Think, if you were able to communicate fairly well through baby talk, how much more accomplished you are now using *real* words to help you say what you are thinking.

Think back to a time when you fled in panic from one or more persons who were waiting to hear you talk. This fear of saying words to others is an emotion common to all of us. With the right practice and know-how, however, anxiety and tension can be easily outwitted. There's no doubt about the value of talk when you want to move ahead in life. When you come to think about it, our society has elevated the act of jogging to an art form or at least to a very polished skill. Jogging can't do half as much for your career as talking can. Why not do it right?

This book will try to help you to use your own everyday language to get along and get ahead in a competitive world. Think about people you know whom you consider "successful" wherever they go. These people seem to exude warmth and confidence, don't they? They *shine* in some way. They seem to know exactly where they are going. There is some shared magic about them. They *like* themselves. Let's see how they do it and what they know.

COPING WITH LANGUAGE:
TALK YOUR WAY TO SUCCESS

CHAPTER I

Using Language to Get Ahead

Everyday Speech Made Simple and Clear

All of us know more than we think. Sometimes you forget this fact and wonder if you know much of anything at all. An instant fear pops into your mind when you are asked to say something in front of one, two, or more persons. You freeze because you are thinking, "I don't know anything about anything." You are really your own worst judge. In the last two years, how many times have you spoken to a group of three or more people at once? More times than you can count. There was the time in the laundromat with Jan and Fred, and the time in your kitchen with the Bridge Club, and all the times at the bowling alley with the gang. So why rate your talk-performances negatively? Why say that you "bombed"? Perhaps you are thinking about all the times your teachers told you that you didn't know very much, that you did poorly in examinations, that you need to try harder, and so on. If only you could have the belief in yourself that Jonathan Livingston Seagull had in himself. He was only a bird, after all, and a mythical one at that.

Consider, for a minute, what you would know even if you had done nothing but *breathe* until you reached your present age. You would know the art of survival. You would have had to communicate your basic needs to someone in order to live as long as you have. And that communication would have had to be clear in order to be understood. With that in mind, think of all the knowledge that has come to you without your even trying. For example, your trusty senses tell you the color, size, shape, texture, and sound of all the objects that surround you. Now think of all you know beyond that, having spent, as most of us do, 45 percent of your time listening, 30 percent speaking, 17 percent reading, and 9 percent writing. Why should you fear to

3

talk? At the bottom of it all is the dread that people won't like you. It is as simple as that.

Your next step, then, is to believe in yourself and to trust your own responses. Small children do it. They reach out to hold us when they are falling; they cry out when they are hungry or angry or ill. They have a "good feeling" about themselves. They *believe* that someone will hear them. Why aren't we as trusting? Well, in the process of growing, we tend to remember the one time that we were disbelieved, or the one person who didn't like the color of our hair, or the one teacher who thought we didn't light up the world. The result is that we have become suspicious, even of ourselves. The idea now is to reaffirm your faith in yourself.

You can do this by thinking of all the things you know about in this wide world. Isn't your brain the most advanced and intricate computer known to mankind? And it works automatically for you. It can store more accurate information than the most sophisticated library in town. Names, faces, facts, numbers, memories, dreams, plans, hopes— all of these are catalogued neatly for you when you need them. The next time you are called upon to "say a few words," or to "make a little speech," just remember to change *speech* to *talk,* and then go on to say something you know. Remember, too, that no one in this world has accumulated the unique knowledge or experiences that you have because they can't have lived your life. Why do we sometimes spend time wishing that we were someone else, when many people might secretly be wishing that they were us?

Every now and then, you hear the complaint that "Life is boring." If only the person who says that would look around. We aren't *capable* of being boring. If everyone in the world walked and talked and looked like everyone else, *then* we might have grounds for talking of boredom. How can boredom be possible, with not one "carbon copy" of anyone else around, even twins? With this in mind, think of your own special gifts and talents, and your unique style. Then open your mouth and say something.

Don't think that what you say doesn't matter. There is nothing you can say that will be totally meaningless. Words have value. They *mean* things. You need to learn how to make words mean all that they *can* mean. Take a moment to think of the words you waste every day.

Haven't you recently said to someone who misread your letter or who misinterpreted your word-signals, "But I meant to say . . ."? Take another look at the words you chose to convey your intended meaning. Did you really say what you meant to say? If you did, no one would ask you to repeat or clarify.

See how poorly words have been used throughout human history. Do you believe, as I do, that all the wars fought since the dawn of civilization happened not because we don't love each other but because the wrong messages were sent? How can we intensely dislike someone on the other side of the world whom we don't know? That is what war is about. It must have something to do with mixing up important signals between nations all over the world.

For example, Paul Revere's message to the citizens of Lexington and Concord depended upon some candles flickering in a church steeple. The poem "Paul Revere's Ride" by Henry Wadsworth Longfellow is a good example of the flow of the communication process. Revere's mission, if you recall, was to warn the local townsfolk that the British were coming to endanger their liberty. He went a step beyond the demand when he opted to tell *how* they were coming, just to be sure of the clarity of his message. Revere instructed his contact in the Old North Church to communicate a full-blown message via the use of a single or double candle light.

> One [candle] if by land
> Two [candles] if by sea
> And I on the opposite shore will be . . .

Didn't Revere take a risk in confiding the translation of so powerful a message to so many people? He knew, as we do, that all messages involve risk, but he believed it a risk worth taking. We all risk something when we take into our hands the responsibility of communication, so we had better make our messages as clear and as simple as we can. Then we won't be asked to restate them. Just imagine the chaos among the townspeople if Paul Revere had to say to his constituents, "Just a minute. You got it wrong. What I meant to say . . ."?

Fortunately, you have the medium of words to speed along your messages. Most of us tend to think that we have to use our own words

"That's One *if by Land,* Two *if by Sea."*

to communicate. That is not necessarily so. Consider that there are special moments in all of our lives, moments of extreme joy or sorrow, when we are too excited to find any words of our own to fit the occasion. Our words lie silent as a lump in our throat. If such is the case, and we find that we must speak despite the emotion, let us not hesitate to call on other people's words when our own fail us. Remember that after President John F. Kennedy was assassinated, Jacqueline Kennedy's grief was so great that she found some small consolation in the memory of words from her husband's favorite musical, *Camelot:*

> Ask all men if they have heard the story
> And tell it loud and clear if they have not
> That once there was a fleeting wisp of glory . . .

While these words were not her own, Mrs. Kennedy knew that they perfectly expressed what the President meant to us as a nation. Perhaps something similar happens to us when we try to express our sorrow to friends at the loss of a loved one. We have so much to say in our hearts, but when we try to utter our deep and profound thoughts, we usually hear ourselves mutter something like "I'm sorry," and let it go at that. In turn, we feel that we have let ourselves settle for something commonplace.

Remember, the people who impress us most speak simply and directly. They avoid talking with overlong words or words that most of us seldom use. When he left the Philippine Islands, General Douglas MacArthur spoke three words that were emblazoned in every one of our childhood history books: "I shall return." You can't ask for greater simplicity than that. Those words meant all that they could mean. MacArthur kept his promise to the Philippine people.

> Next to breathing,
> speech is the most universal activity.

Communicating with Confidence

We all admire people who appear confident. You know, however, that appearances can be deceiving. Talking in front of even two people can be a terrifying experience. It *can* be unless you know the numerous tricks that professional talkers, including newscasters, politicians, actors, teachers, and real estate agents, know. Let us trace the fear pattern as it grows, or is imagined, in your mind.

Why do you have all the confidence you need when you are talking to your plants or your cat in the kitchen? Because you are in a cozy, familiar place, surrounded by objects of your personal affection. To those objects, you can do no wrong. Your words dance from your mouth. They are often delightful, because unguarded and spontaneous. Often, too, they spill over from one thought or idea to the next. These separate "jumps" are frequently unrelated to each other or even to the world of common sense. There is no anxiety in your bones.

Consider now the next step on the speechfright ladder. You are in a more formal setting. Let's say that you have been invited to spend some hours of casual conversation at a friend's house in a Vermont ski resort. You know that six people will be there, and you are already friends with two of them. That means you must meet four new faces. What will you say? Will they like you? Will you like them? You will, of course, be expected to say something. Will it be the right thing? For a partial answer to these questions, look back to the preceding pages of this chapter. Believe in your worth. Look at it this way. You are worth knowing because you are an extraordinary individual. Ask yourself what you have done lately that is important to you. Perhaps you have planted a new vegetable garden, run in the marathon, seen a few Norman Rockwell paintings or the latest Woody Allen film, volunteered for action in some community service. What you have accomplished may seem small and insignificant to you, but how you tell about it can be dynamite. For an added conversational edge, find out what the others in your group have been into lately. Asking people to talk about themselves is the shy person's key to success. It also relieves the pressure on you and takes you off the hook for the moment.

The next stage in the progression of the talkfright syndrome is the more formal situation, like the PTA meeting, where you don't know everyone and might not care about ever knowing them. You wish you could lie down and die. Well, don't. Remember that you know more than you think. If you have agreed to talk at a meeting of this sort, remind yourself how perfectly noble you were to accept the invitation in the first place. Then think of all the cowardly people who might have been asked to talk but made up the flimsy excuse of having to lose three wisdom teeth to the cause of dental surgery. How highly you must be regarded by others to have been nominated for this exalted post. People are lucky for the chance to listen to you. After all this, if you still find yourself attacked by your nervous system, as all talkers everywhere are, you should remember that this seizure of the self is perfectly normal and can be dealt with by some easy home remedies. The first remedy is to face yourself and admit that no one has ever been known to collapse and die from talkfright. The second remedy is to begin immediate breathing exercises that will enable you to breathe yourself into a calm. To do this you must inhale as much air as you possibly can. Feel it coursing down into the diaphragm, the ready-made pit just above your belt-line. Here is a simple exercise that is helpful in putting on your natural brakes.

Inhale to the count of three.
Exhale to the count of four.
Inhale to the count of five.
Exhale to the count of six.
And so on.

This exercise gradually expands the amount of oxygen in your system. The overall effect is one of induced calmness. You must remember that no talker is ever completely calm, and this is a wonderful thing. If you are too serene, you would probably have a limp, monotonous voice that would put everyone, including yourself, to sleep. You can't outwit your nervous system, but you can befriend it and understand how it works for you.

Everyone who has ever talked before a group of any size has experienced the following symptoms: cold, clammy palms that "leak" uncontrollably, knees that bang together like cymbals, a stomach like an elevator, and a heartbeat that drowns out thunder. All these symptoms indicate that you are normal and anxious to please your audience. In turn, the audience always appreciates your effort, because they know that they would find it just as difficult if they were in your shoes. *You,* however, are the one who stands before them, and that thought alone should offer you a warm glow of achievement. In the last analysis, it is the person who *does,* rather than the person who *is,* who achieves the highest and best rewards in life. This should push you to the podium or the head table, where you can look out upon a sea of smiling faces and know that your words are making a difference to them. After all, being gripped is better than being touched. A hug is better than a handshake. You can hug your audience with your eyes, and they will feel it no less.

For your own improvement, why not make a list of speakers you have heard who "turned you on." What qualities in their voice or person made you like them? Have you noticed that the voice reflects personality and temperament? A well-adjusted, happy person is likely to have a sparkling voice with many different vocal ranges, or "ups and downs." Listen to some radio announcers or disc jockeys. Remember that the voice alone is all you have to judge these personalities by. Haven't you often experienced the fantasy of imagining what a radio celebrity looks like on the basis of the mellowness or stridency of his voice? And haven't you often been amazed at how different the person looks from the way his voice makes him seem? Frequently, a burly, husky, booming voice belongs to a thin, short person. The particular personal character that voices reveal is that of confidence or lack of it. A phone call from you and your voice could be enough to clinch a deal or call it off. Never underestimate the power of the word well spoken, in good order, for the greatest effect. Let us look at some people we know who communicate with confidence.

"I Know We Have to Stop Meeting Like This, but I Just Love Your Voice."

Popularity polls have been taken from time to time that help to determine which public communicators reach the most people. When you watch the news on television, what kind of talk do you look for in the anchorperson? Surely you don't appreciate someone who goes beyond reporting facts and interjects personal opinion into the story. Should newspeople be encouraged to interpret the facts as well as report them? Does any kind of frivolous conversation lessen their personal credibility?

One of the most admired reporters today is veteran newscaster Walter Cronkite. Polls continually show him in the lead with regard to credibility, integrity, sympathy, sincerity. It has been shown that if Cronkite were to tell us that the world as we know it would come to a screeching halt tomorrow, we would probably accept such gruesome news more readily from him than from anyone else. Why? He does not have a "movie star" face, but he does have a secret ingredient called credibility, which enables us to trust his judgment simply because he has never let us down. People always believe someone until they have reason not to. When Cronkite says "And that's the way it is . . ." at the close of his television program each night, we *know* that around the world things are as he says they are. The Greeks had a word for this quality of character in a person. They called it *ethos,* which means that the person who says something is as important as *what* he says. How the listener sees or perceives the talker determines how easily the listener is influenced.

The Kennedy family has produced many speakers who communicate with confidence. President John Kennedy's words have become legend at a time when national crises seem to be assaulting us on all sides:

Ask not what your country can do for you;
ask what you can do for your country.

Attorney General Robert F. Kennedy reminded us that

some men see things as they are and ask why.
I dream things that never were and say why not.

Both of these brothers were able to move multitudes through the power of talk, that is, through the right words spoken at the right time. Listen to the words of Senator Edward M. Kennedy in his first public address following his brother Robert's assassination:

If there was one great meaning to Robert Kennedy's campaign, one ideal that fired the consciousness of this nation in 1968, it was that voting every four years was not enough to make a citizen . . .

In these words you can hear the thundering voice of the Senator as it rings with new hope for the people. He is making us *reach* to the height of his words. It would have been easier for him to say that people should do more than just vote; they should ease the suffering of their neighbors and become less selfish. You can *feel* the difference when words are chosen carefully. They have a power and a magic that makes you want to march to their music. Napoleon often said that if he heard the right words he would go to war. In other words, people can charm us, through words, into doing what they want.

The slain civil rights leader Martin Luther King was another fine example of someone who communicated with confidence. Where he could have said that he hoped for all oppressed people to be free some day, he relied upon the simplicity of the repeated word to carry his message like a poem or a prayer:

> I have a dream today.
> I have a dream that one day every valley shall be exalted,
> every hill and mountain shall be made low . . .

King further underscored his plea for racial equality and his belief in American democracy when he used the words of someone else through his recitation of the patriotic verse "My country, 'tis of thee." It is a proven persuasive strategy to choose familiar words and repeat them in a new context.

To communicate with confidence you must believe in your own worth, say something you feel strongly about in the best possible way, and trust that your hearers will value your honesty. Do you have a good reason for suffering the pain of being scared and the bother of hiding it in the first place?

Is the Message Sent the Message Received?

> Talking and eloquence are not the same:
> to speak, and to speak well, are two things.
>
> —Ben Jonson

How do our messages get bungled? Why can an idea be so clear in our mind and the translation of it so obscure when it issues from our mouth? To help clarify the process of communication, a communication specialist, Claude E. Shannon, in his book with Warren Weaver, *The Mathematical Theory of Communication,* has provided a diagram that can be adapted to trace the life of a spoken thought from inspiration to expiration.

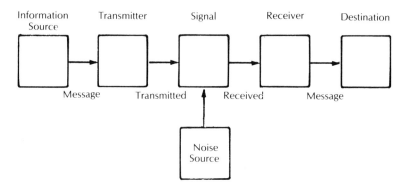

Although Shannon's model was designed for computer communication, it is flexible enough to accommodate the human process.

Let's try to work the model out in practical terms. When a spontaneous idea originates in your mind, which is the information source of all messages, that idea is in its purest form. It is precise, correct, unspoiled, clear. This is because you think in images or symbols. You don't think in words. At this point in the communication scheme, the message is 100 percent intact. You begin to run into trouble, however, when the messsage slips into your mouth and is ready to be spoken. Notice that between the information source (brain) and the transmitter (vocal cords), the message has to be encoded, or put into a word pattern that matches the meaning in your mind. This is difficult to do, because you often lack the right words to pin the message down properly. In whatever shape it's in, the transmitted message is changed into the signal, which is the sound made by the vocal chords as they release the word into the air.

Sometimes you stammer and stutter while your mind frantically searches for the proper word to express your message. All of this deliberation goes on at ultrahigh speed, so that we are not aware of time lags. When the words finally pop out, they are frequently unsuited to the idea and you are disappointed. Worse, there is no time to retrieve the words or to exchange them for better ones. This is the spot where communication can become lazy. You have to make do with the vocabulary your mind sent you because it is all you have to work with. Don't worry over this. The words you already know can be made to serve well if you work at it.

The noise source can also distort an essentially simple message. The noise box is where all kinds of unwanted sounds are added to your signal. These sounds were not planned by the information source when the message got started. They disturb the flow of language like snow in a poor television picture. Considering all the noise (distractions) around us and within us, it is amazing that any kind of communication ever takes place. Because of these interferences, it is good to be mindful that when two or more people converse, misunderstanding is the rule; understanding is a happy accident.

How, exactly, does the noise factor serve to disrupt your message? For one thing, it comes at you from two directions, internal and external, or inside and outside. External noise factors are constant companions in life. You can't control them. You may say that you are unaware of them, but that is not the case. You are dimly aware of them at all times. These noises come from your environment. They are many and varied. For example, outside the home, office, or classroom are the motors of planes flying overhead, trucks spouting fumes on the parkway, electrical storms, sirens of fire engines, and crowds on the street talking and laughing. Inside buildings the noise is even more pronounced because it is closer to you. Above your head is the low buzz of the electric light. In your midst are people talking, children calling out. There is the television, radio, sewing machine, stereo, dishwasher, perhaps a domestic argument next door, and, of course, people simply moving about. All of this noise is external. Much of it can be going on all at once. You say that you can tune it out, but that is nearly impossible because there is so much of it. In fact, you are put off by it. It is one of the reasons for all those aspirin commercials on television.

As if external noise weren't enough, you are continually besieged by a barrage of internal noise, that is, noise that happens inside your head. You daydream a lot, and these pleasant messages tend to disturb messages coming to you from other people. Think of this: you are never really 100 percent anywhere at any time. If you realize this, you won't be unduly discouraged because you are doing "what comes naturally." If you *were* 100 percent present at every occasion or commitment, you would be superhuman and probably impossible to live with. Consider your normal, routine day. You plan things privately, in your head, all day long. You think of your future, your past, the confrontation you had with your boss or your teacher, an argument at home, a job interview coming up, a date for Saturday night. To add to this, you are also time-oriented. You live by your watch. You have a built-in time clock that goes off in your head the moment one task has ended and another begins. Think about how you felt when classes were almost over. The clock said five minutes to go. You shuffled papers, moved around a lot in your seat, became generally restless and ready to move on to the next obligation. Psychologically, you had already left the room at this point. Nothing is heard or learned after your clock stops.

All of these noises, plus a few extras, like a toothache, headache, or sore throat, serve to deflect words coming from or at you from their original intent. When you think of all these distractions, the business of communicating takes place more smoothly than seems possible. That we get through at all is the wonder.

The last leg of the message-journey has to do with the hearer or receiver of your words. If you want to be absolutely certain that your words are heard as you intended, you should place the person you are talking to in a soundproof booth. There, at least, no external noises would compete with your words. However, you would still have to do battle with the noise factors in the person's head. So the cycle goes round and round. Take heart, and keep striving to unclutter the channels as much as possible.

Here is a simple illustration of what can happen when only one word-message travels from one person to another. Imagine that the parallel columns you see pictured are adjacent high-rise apartment buildings. A neighbor on the top floor shouts an urgent message for help. This signal is not interpreted correctly by the receiver. It quickly becomes distorted. The third neighbor changes the message even more,

Is the Message Sent the Message Received?

and by the time it reaches the ears of the fourth person it bears no resemblance to the original message.

You have played similar games at parties. A sentence is whispered into the ear of the first person, who in turn repeats it to the next person, and so on. The last uttering of the sentence usually bears little resemblance to the original version. Here we can forgive poor communication because it is a game. What most of us don't realize is that much real-life communication is not very different. You shouldn't be surprised, then, as your thoughts come to rest in the mind (destination) of the receiver, if they bear little resemblance to what you meant when your information source first activated the circuit.

Is There Communication When You Talk?

The next time you have a chance, be sure to observe two people speaking with each other in a restaurant, school, subway, or street. Ask yourself if one is talking and the other listening, or if one is talking and the other waiting to talk. Are you looking at two "talking heads," or is something truly significant going on between those two people?

It is impossible *not* to communicate with others all day long. You can do it poorly, but even a shrug of the shoulders or a handshake tells you all you need to know about someone else. Even somebody who sulks all day is communicating quite well. A person who shouts or argues is doing well, too. At least his message is clear. No one doubts what he is saying or *not* saying.

You can spot the people who are getting through to each other by the way they walk and stand, by the way they pick things up and hold them in their hand. When someone is "pouring out his heart" to you, do you look around the room and wave to people you know? The successful person is a respectful listener. He or she listens with the eyes more than the ears. There is only a marginal level of communication going on when you avoid looking into the center of another's eyes. Eyes are the windows of the mind. Even when the tongue is silent, the eyes can and do speak volumes.

The next time someone greets you, try standing still, looking the person in the eyes, and answering the greeting. How quickly we rush on and are half way down the block before we think of acknowledging a greeting. It is such a simple way to make and keep friends.

To talk more effectively, there are several rules that govern success.

1. Know what you want to say; understand your own thoughts. Remember, you can only say one thing at a time. Be sure that your own mind is clear before you talk.

2. Say your words distinctly. Don't slur the pronunciation of any part of a word. Here are some examples of "shortcuts" that make for slovenly speech:

I've lived in the Nited States of Merica my tire life. Instead of:
I've lived in the United States of America my entire life.

Those who are careless with the middle of word sounds might be heard to say:

It was a wunnerful pome but her reading runed it. Instead of:
It was a wonderful poem but her reading ruined it.

Word endings very often get chopped off because we are in such a rush. We tend to say:

The secon' han' on the clock wouldn' go. Instead of:
The second hand on the clock wouldn't go.

3. Pronounce your words according to the best dictionary standards. You'd be surprised how often everyday words are mispronounced by the most educated people. Beware, this is a mark of your own taste. It is an effort to track a word down in the dictionary when you aren't sure how it should sound, but the rewards of good speech are worth it. For example, you may find yourself being interviewed for a job and you keep mispronouncing the word "recognize."

Hello, Mr. Stewart. I dint recanize ya at first.
Glad ta meetcha.

If you forget that there's a "cog" in recognize, it won't shorten your life, but that isn't the point. What matters in getting ahead is that you have acquired the *habit* or *pattern* of good talk. It is the overall cumulative effect that either sells you at a high price or sells you short. Many a job promotion has been lost because the candidate had a recurrent pattern of shoddy speech. Would you enthusiastically promote someone who answered your business telephone sounding like Carol Burnett's Mrs. Wiggins character? Here's a telephone sequence that might refresh your memory:

Caller: Hello.
Mrs. Wiggins: Yeah.
Caller: May I speak with Mr. Tudball?
Mrs. Wiggins: Naw. He ain't in. (She files her nails).
Caller: When do you expect him back?
Mrs. Wiggins: Who knows? I only work here.

This dialogue may seem farfetched, but there are people who run a close second to these fictional characters. Such people can't possibly achieve the level of success that belongs to the articulate, confident, well-poised person.

Here are some words that are commonly mispronounced:

pumpkin	We say punkin. This is in the same league as "chicken pops" instead of chicken pox.
chasm	We forget that the "ch" sound is "k."
letter	We say ledda.
probably	We say proly or probly.
genuine	We add some *wine* to the word. There shouldn't be any.
comparable	Remember that the stressed syllable is the first one.

Many of us add unwanted syllables to words. Here are some examples:

The burgular jumped down the chiminey in search of a fillum for the picanic. Instead of:

The burglar jumped down the chimney in search of a film for the picnic.

Some sentences become cluttered and untidy through the addition of a single "misfit" letter:

I see him acoming down the road.
The child was ascared of the dark.
Take ahold of my hand.
I'm ahoping to win the contest with my especial entry.

4. Speak without affectation. We all know the classic example of the highbrow actress who addresses everyone as "Dahling," walks with a glide, and sports a foot-long cigarette holder for better smoke rings. A funny character indeed. Aren't there some equivalents in real life? Ourselves, perhaps? Whenever you have to talk before even a small group, isn't there the chance that you become "someone else"? You assume a different voice to cover over your own trembling one. Why bother? The simplest way of dealing with this problem is to admit to your nerves attacking you, take the deepest breath possible, and go on.

Tell yourself that there are many examples of personalities who have cultivated an affected or false voice. Listen to the major radio stations and you'll hear seven out of ten announcers who sound just like one another, as if they all attended the same school of broadcasting. Often, too, people in the ministry tend to falsify their voices for effect when they preach. They either deliver their sermons a few notes too high and sound like a soprano, or too low and sound like a frog. The best way to foil the desire to put on an act is to tell yourself that you are in your best form when you are not trying to impress. Overkill comes from overdoing.

5. Phrase your words in their natural order, with slight pauses to make your meaning clear. Words are strung like beads on a chain, and not all of them have the same weight. Some should be emphasized because they carry more meaning. For example, when Winston Churchill said,

I have nothing to offer but blood, toil, tears and sweat . . .

he had to place deliberate emphasis on bending his words in the right order to convey the greatest meaning. If an orchestra leader were to conduct Churchill's words, they might read like this on the music sheet:

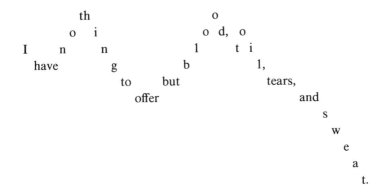

The voice is, after all, the most precise wind instrument known to mankind.

6. Emphasize certain important or key words that will give your talk character and persuasiveness. As a general rule, it helps if you downplay the adjectives and prepositions and emphasize nouns and verbs. Repetition of a key word or phrase is also useful.

Here is a short passage from the pen of Daniel Webster. The words are bold enough to leap from the page with the proper vocal force.

Let our object be our country, our whole country, and nothing but our country. And by the blessing of God, may that country itself become a vast and splendid monument, not of oppression and terror, but of wisdom, of peace and of liberty, upon which the world may gaze with admiration forever.

To develop good talk-habits, find paragraphs written by orators or statesmen that contain a degree of color and mark up the paragraphs to suit your personality. Develop a shorthand of signs and symbols for your own use. Then decide how you want to break up the paragraph to provide the greatest meaning. Here are some suggestions for the shorthand approach:

_____	underline for intensity
( )	circle word for pause or stop
/ / /	stop after phrase

Your marked-up practice sheet might look something like this:

Let our object be our (country,) our whole (country,)
and nothing but our (country) / / / And by the blessing
of (God,) may that country itself / / / become a vast and
splendid monument, / / / not of oppression and terror, / / /
but of wisdom, of peace and of (liberty,) / / / upon which
the world may gaze with admiration (forever.)

7. Be earnest, vivacious, alive when you talk. It will make your language interesting and give it color. Do not talk too fast. Always make yourself enunciate clearly with phrasing and expression.

Fast talkers, or "motor-mouths," tend to burn out their candle quickly. You will have more *style* in your voice if you take time to practice exercises like this one:

I had eighteen bottles of whiskey in my cellar and was told by my wife to empty the contents of each and every bottle down the sink, or else. . . . I said I would and proceeded with the unpleasant task.

I withdrew the cork from the first bottle and poured the contents down the sink with the exception of one glass which I drank. I extracted the cork from the second bottle and did likewise with it with the exception of one glass which I drank.

I then withdrew the cork from the third bottle and poured the whiskey down the sink which I drank. I pulled the cork from the fourth bottle down the sink and poured the bottle down the glass which I drank.

I pulled the bottle from the cork of the next and drank the sink out of it, and the rest down the glass. I pulled the sink out of the next glass and poured the cork down the bottle. Then I corked the sink with the glass, bottled the drink, and drank the pour. When I had emptied everything, I steadied the house with one hand, counted the glasses, corks, bottles, and sinks with the other hand which were twenty-nine, and as the house came by, I counted them again, and finally had all the houses in one bottle, which I drank.

—Anonymous

If you speak this passage properly, the strange displacements of words will automatically slow you down. And as for meaning, it is built right into the piece. Just go with the flow and you will find that you really are the colorful character in the tale.

8. When given a selection written by someone else, be sure to study it and understand it. Be sure that you have caught the mood of the author. Try to interpret the piece emotionally as well as intellectually.

Here is a good practice exercise designed by the best "talker" of all time, William Shakespeare. Prince Hamlet instructs the Players he has hired "to catch the conscience of the King." He warns them against affectation or phoniness in their speech:

Speak the speech, I pray you, as I pronounced it to you, trippingly on the tougue; but if you mouth it, as many of our players do, I had as lief the town-crier spoke my lines. Nor do not saw the air too much with your hand, thus; but use all gently, for in the very torrent, tempest, and (as I may say) whirlwind of your passion, you must acquire and beget a temperance that may give it smoothness. O it offends me to the soul to hear a robustious periwig-pated fellow tear a passion to tatters, to very rags, to split the ears of the groundlings, who for the most part are capable of nothing but inexplicable dumb-shows and noise. I would have such a fellow whipped for o'er-doing Termagant. It out-herods Herod: pray you, avoid it.

Whenever you must resort to "speaking a speech," be sure that you first understand exactly what the words mean in their simplest form. Underline every word you don't understand and look up its meaning. For example, in the above passage, these words seem to be most difficult:

lief—here it means "sooner" or "preferred."
robustious—burly, forceful.
periwig—long, white-curled official wig used by members of the British court.
groundlings—spectators who bought the cheapest seats in the pit of the theater. They were usually a noisy group, given to throwing fruit and jeering at the actors.
Termagant—an ancient god, shown in literature as a raging bull.
Herod—loud-mouthed biblical king who was notorious for ranting and raving.

After definitions of words have been settled, take whole phrases and see if there are any lapses of meaning in them. What about "tear a passion to tatters"? Doesn't it imply that emotions are best conveyed when they are not forced? You can't pretend an emotion you don't feel. The overall message of Hamlet's advice to the players is that if you "mouth" an important talk, you are simply going through the motions of saying empty words in a loud voice, without any emotional commitment. They ring hollow, as if you had memorized several isolated words without bothering to investigate their meaning. Also implied in Hamlet's warning is the danger of making random gestures ("saw the air") and of shouting at lung-top for extra effect. The effect of shouting is disastrous and deafening.

The Power of Positive Speech

> Know you how much the people may be moved
> By that which he will utter?
>   —Shakespeare

We have discussed how impossible it is *not* to communicate. We need to know how to communicate well, because "common" talk often is not enough for success in our demanding, competitive society. Since you talk for many hours each day, you might as well make an effort to go a step beyond the demand. You might outwit the mediocre talker. You will not need any of the following advice if you plan to go into hiding or become a hermit and live in a cave. However, if your place is among the people of this town, state, or universe, you had best sharpen your ability to do what comes naturally better than nature intended. These words are for people who sell Volkswagens, that their sales may pick up. They are for Avon saleswomen, that more doors may open to them. They are for telephone talkers, and fast talkers, for auctioneers and airline stewardesses, for photographers and construction crews, courtiers and kings.

All of us like someone who has a pleasant personality. By personality we usually mean the effect of someone's total behavior on us. Think about it, and you will find that the people who are easy to like are generally "upbeat," positive, and optimistic in the presentation of themselves. They are exposed to the same setbacks and advances as everyone is, but they seem to emerge victorious from even the most unfortunate situations. Why is this? It's because they know how to accept each day without getting all knotted up inside. They are happy to be alive, and any other good thing that happens is a bonus for the day. They have developed a habit of coping, which comes from a lot of hard work and the determination to live one's life as happily as possible.

Contrary, how many people speak only of negative subjects: illness, bad weather, unfaithful friends, disloyal children, crime, disaster. When you say, "Hello. How are you?," the standard response is usually, "Don't ask." Or:

I'm glad you asked. I've been miserable. My pesty sister keeps calling me, and I don't have time for her. My air conditioner broke down and I have to sit in this small crampy apartment and die of the heat. I have a toothache that never lets up, and my cat ate the goldfish.

Some people can tell the saddest tales imaginable. They must work on them around the clock. People like this are apt to remain lonely and be shunned by the rest of the world. How much better it is to speak positively, to say "yes" more than "no," "I will" rather than "I won't," "I can" instead of "impossible," "too soon," not "too late." How do you acquire the skill of using positive language? There are a number of ways. You can learn to speak positively by following ten simple rules of good talk.

1. The successful talker has developed powers of sharp observation. This means that the ordinary transactions of the day become a field of research. We all watch other people. Why not do it for fun and profit? Don't lose any chance you have to study people in detail. Try to remember what kind of clothes they are wearing. Notice how they stand. Do they hop from one foot to another? Do they look off into the distance when someone talks to them? Do they touch each other? Be especially observant in places of public transportation, such as bus or train stations. When you enter a train, look at the people opposite you. Are they *pretending* to read the newspaper or are they really absorbed in it? Observe those who are engaged in conversation. If you look closely, you can estimate the degree of their friendship.

How does this attention to detail help our speech progress? For one thing, it accustoms you to paying heed to other people, and so you become less selfish and self-centered. For another, if you remember something special and positive about everyone you meet, you are on the road to becoming a successful personality. Something special might mean a particular manner of speech or a type of smile or frown. It might mean a certain style in clothes or the kind of companions a person is with. Something positive might include, most especially, remembering the name of someone you were just introduced to. Few things make people happier than hearing their own name spoken. This is also a nice way for people to remember you. A potential employer might think:

> You remembered my name. You must be good at other things, too, like remembering to be on time and remembering to greet my customers by name and remembering to carry out all the jobs I've lined up for the day.

An easy way to recall names is to associate a particular trait or place or object with the person. For example, perhaps Robert Redford stands near a *red* chair or wears a *red* jacket. Jot down *red* as your key to his face. The next time you meet the person you'll make the connection.

2. The successful talker has built up a broad background of knowledge in the areas in which he wants to communicate. Remember, you know more than you think you do. To keep yourself on top, open all your senses to acquiring as much information as possible in your areas of interest. Read, or at least browse through, best sellers in your field. You can always drop an author's name or an idea from the book at just the right moment. You should also know a broad spectrum of current events, for the purpose of enhancing your own credibility. For example, if you are attending a business luncheon and you don't know that there has been a major earthquake in California, or you never heard of the plight of the DC-10 aircraft, you aren't likely to be taken seriously in other matters.

3. The successful talker has developed the capacity for thinking logically. All good ideas have a beginning, a middle, and an end. Dialogue shouldn't sound like a worn-out record that skips over several grooves before it picks up the music again. Although all purposeful talk contains some degree of loose thinking, it is best to avoid as much foggy discourse as you can. Clear, easy-to-understand speech will automatically boost your personal credit rating. Understanding how to think and talk logically helps you to cut through problems. Because the process of rational thought is so complicated, it would be well to know some of the most common errors in organized talk.

a. The hasty generalization. Here you lump everything you are trying to prove under a single heading. For example, if you say that all redheads have hot tempers, you are stepping out of a logical frame. All the redheads you know may indeed fly off the handle, but you can't speak for every redhead the world over. In order for people to believe us, we must adjust our statements to mean something plausible. Otherwise, people will take us at face value. They will distrust our sincerest efforts to communicate with them.

b. The faulty premise. The premise is the basic idea around which a thought revolves. When the premise is faulty we are looking at only one facet of an issue. Some examples of faulty premises are statements like:

i. Football promotes unselfishness. Unselfishness, shown in strong team spirit, is a worthy by-product of any sports program, but it is not the reason for playing the game. Football may also promote selfishness if players are determined to win by fair or foul means.

ii. High taxes cause inflation. You often hear people argue with statements like this one. They try to paint the whole picture-problem in one pat statement. How much more believable it is to say something like:

This inflation is really getting to me. I wonder,
if taxes were lowered, would the problem abate a
little?

c. The hidden premise. This false argument assumes that the hearer understands what prejudices are behind the speaker's words. For example, when someone says, "Billy is retarded. Don't listen to him," that person is implying that mentally slow children aren't worth listening to. When you hear the statement, "That camera was made in Japan. I won't buy it," you know the speaker thinks that nothing good comes from Japan.

d. Equivocation. This is an intentional shift in the meaning of key terms in order to throw the listener off base. For example, a potential destroyer of our constitutional rights may be said to be a revisionist rather than an unruly malcontent. In this category the word "chauvinist" would belong. While today the word has come to have strong negative overtones, its original meaning was "super-patriot." It applied to those who were fierce defenders of the flag.

e. The post hoc fallacy. This Latin phrase stands for an argument which says that because one event preceded another it caused the second event to happen. An example of this type of faulty judgment might sound something like this:

Grandma: The picture tube in the television seems to be out.
Grandpa: Why are you looking at me?
Grandma: Because you watched it last. I went to bed early last
           night.

Grandpa: What do you mean by that?
Grandma: What do you think I mean? The television was working just fine when I watched my soap operas yesterday.
Grandpa: Are you telling me that I broke it?
Grandma: You said it. I didn't.

f. Insufficient evidence. There is usually not enough evidence, or proof, behind much of what we say. That is why people argue a lot. In order to be as believable as possible, we should try to prove, through fact, not fancy, what we mean when we make certain statements. An insufficient-evidence conversation might sound something like this:

Jan: Don't vote for Willy for student council president.
Pam: Why not?
Jan: Because he doesn't know how to run anything.
Pam: He seems to be capable. Everyone likes him.
Jan: Look, running for office is a political game. Look at the Watergate crowd. They're all crooks. Everyone in government is on the take. Why should Willy be any different?

Other faults in reasoning include the use of such claims as: "All college courses are a waste of time." If possible, avoid the use of "all" or "every." It could prove embarrassing when it comes to backing up your statements with hard, cold evidence.

4. The successful talker appreciates his capabilities and recognizes his limitations. It is better to stress one's strong points rather than dwell on weaknesses. How can you know your abilities? These questions can help you to rate your own talk-effectiveness:

Do you like to be around people?
Do you enjoy talking with them?
Does anybody have difficulty understanding you? Do they ask you to repeat what you say?
Do you really try to be understood?
Do you look up the correct pronunciation of words you aren't sure of, or at least substitute a word you know for one you don't know?
Do you look at people when you talk to them?

Is your facial expression flexible enough to change with shifting conversation?

Are you aware that the power of good body posture makes for better
communication situations?

Do you think before you speak, or speak before you think? Do you
say with the poet, "How can I know what I think till I see what
I say?"

With the exception of the third and last questions, if you answered
"yes" to the queries, you have already cultivated many fine habits of
talk. People would like to be around you. You are sincere and open.
You try to please, and others try to please you.

As for your limitations, whatever they are, there's a trick to help
you sweep them under the rug. If you concentrate hard on making
your good points even better, your weak spots will scarcely be noticed
or heard. They will become so insignificant that no one will be aware
of them. In order to sharpen your best skills, seize as many opportunities
as you can to participate in talk situations. The practice will add the
polish you need.

Here is a suggestion for setting up ways to learn and practice better
vocal techniques. Watch as many television talk shows as you can in
one week. Tune in to Dick Cavett, Phil Donohue, Barbara Walters,
Johnny Carson, Tom Snyder, Dinah Shore, William F. Buckley. Watch
each of their styles closely. How do they treat their listeners? Remember,
these hosts were hired because they can talk well and listen well. Take
note of the kinds of questions they ask their guests. Are they general,
personal, or a mixture of both? How does the host react when a guest
refuses to respond to a question? Every good talk-show star has a built-
in alarm in his or her head that goes off when things aren't going
well. Like a magician, he must turn the discussion sometimes full circle
until he has regained the confidence of his guest. The talk stars of
the air waves must be ready for any kind of unpleasant situation. They
must cope with rough spots as we cope with traffic jams. If they "blew
their cool," nothing at all would get done. They know, instead, that
there is a way to reach everyone, even the coldest and least approachable.

5. The successful talker has an accurate picture of the people he is

talking to. It is essential to know many things about the people one is going to communicate with. We must know the reason the audience has for coming together to hear us. Every listener to every talker shares the same question: "What's in this for me?"

If your hearers are generally composed of all ages, a general talk is advisable. Never risk boredom! If you must talk to adults and children at once, be sure to speak moderately and briefly. Children become restless. If, on the other hand, you are sharing conversation with a room full of eighteen-year-olds, you have free rein over this tightly knit group. They will accept you for what you are. A homogeneous audience is usually easier to reach and easier to sustain than a mixed group.

The level of education in any group is apparent from physical appearance. People with higher education tend to sit still and listen more attentively than those without many years of formal schooling. In addition, words alone—that is, message content—are usually sufficient for the better-educated listener. Other groups rely more on visual supports to words, such as pictures and charts. They also like color and movement.

How our listeners act also gives a clue to how they feel about us. There are three main types of behavior groups:

a. Receptive—Easy to reach, warm, open.
b. Hostile—Difficult to reach because they are angry. These people can be converted. It all depends on our skill.
c. Apathetic—Most difficult to reach because they are indifferent. With them, we have a double challenge. We must wake them up and warm them up. Every listener has the capacity to change.

6. The successful talker realizes the power of personality in communication. Your personality is unique enough for people to remember you forever. We call entertainers "personalities" because they trust themselves to stand before us as they are.

Your personality has a power of its own. Find out if your special talent lies in a formal or an informal style of talk. If talking with small groups is your forte, cultivate that gift until it becomes an art for you.

7. The successful talker will use every opportunity for practice. The key to talking well is practice. When the woman on the subway asked the young man carrying a violin case how she could get to Carnegie Hall, he replied, "Practice, lady, practice."

The first step in practice is to do some warm-up exercises, much as

"Enchanted to Meet You."

dancers or musicians do before shows. For the best-intentioned talker, these exercises start with deep, concentrated breathing. They take only a few minutes to do. Here are some ideas:

a. Stand comfortably erect. Place the palms of your hands over your diaphragm (the muscle just above your belt-line) so that your middle fingertips meet. Breathe in through your mouth, forcing the fingertips apart.

b. Pant like a dog. Feel how your body expands and contracts in the region of the diaphragm.

c. Place one hand above your diaphragm in front, and the other just about opposite on your back. Breathe in, noticing the body expansion in the front and back. Exhale, noticing the contraction before and after.

d. Place your hand above your diaphragm. As you breathe in, notice the outward expansion of the abdominal muscles. As you breathe out, prolong the sound of "sssssss." This hissing sound should be smooth and even. Notice the gradual push inward of the abdominal cavity as you exhale.

e. Using the same expansion and contraction of the abdominal muscles and diaphragm, whisper the vowel sounds: ah, ay, ee, aw, oh, oo. Extend each vowel sound for the count of ten. Repeat the exercise saying the vowels out loud. Work for a smooth, easily sustained tone. Control your outgoing breath so that the end of the vowel (at the count of ten) is as full, clear, and without strain as the beginning of the sound.

f. Inhale easily and imperceptibly. As you exhale, begin to say the alphabet, letting the sounds glide smoothly on the exhaled breath.

g. Gradually increase the number of letters you can say smoothly.

These exercises are a vital part of practice because you can't speak well if you don't breathe correctly. Most of us think that we know how to breathe because we've been doing it without effort all our lives. The fact is, if we leave all to nature, we become flabby of voice, just as we become flabby of body without exercise.

You know that you aren't breathing properly when you become out of breath easily and are fatigued around the middle of the day. When this happens, it means that you are talking from your throat. You have forgotten to take that big dip of air that reaches down to your waistline. For a lesson on good breathing technique, watch a dog, cat, or baby sleeping. See how the diaphragm is the center of their deep breaths. This means that they are totally relaxed, at peace, with no tension or anxiety. If you take a few seconds out of your busy schedule for deep breathing, you will find yourself less tense and less anxious than you thought possible. All this calmness is yours without even popping a pill. The brain and body do it all.

After you have finished your breathing exercises, you are ready to practice your words. Look at your notes or outline. Read it over to yourself silently so that your mind locks in the meaning. Once the meaning is settled to your satisfaction, you are ready to say your words out loud. This gives you the chance to hear the sound of the words as they leave your mouth. You can catch any bumpy phrases or sentences here. Look at the words on your page or index cards and imprint them in your mind. Don't memorize. Just be on friendly terms with the words.

While you are practicing alone, it is best to have a room to yourself. As you become more familiar with your script, gradually raise your eyes from the page and let them focus on some inanimate object, such as a lampshade, water faucet, light bulb, or bedpost. You are not expecting a response from this "audience," but it does give you confidence in delivery as you become free of the page. Later, when the bedpost and light bulb are replaced with real people, you won't be as nervous looking at them because you have included "looking up" as part of your practice. How often should your eyes leave your script? A good rule of thumb is to let your eyes come to rest on your listeners at least twice as much as they rest on your notes.

After you have practiced with your lifeless objects, you are ready for the real thing. Find a friend who will listen to you with a critical ear. Remember, a true friend is one who tells you the truth. If your words lack vitality to your friend, sit down and do some serious revision.

8. The successful talker recognizes the importance of physical elements in talk. Physical energy is vital in carrying off your words. So much meaning is conveyed through the body. Hidden messages come across before a person ever opens his mouth. Take a look at recruiting posters the Armed Forces use to attract candidates for military service. Not a word is spoken, or needs to be, on a poster, but the physical representation of the young soldier tells all. You see his rugged jaw, arms clasped behind his back for emphasis, heels together and toes three inches apart. The unwritten message says: "Join this guy, and you'll have character, loyalty, courage, honesty." Imagine the effect on us if the chap in the poster were sitting cross-legged on a sailboat, dangling a fishing rod and wearing jeans with several dozen patches.

When you talk, the moves your body makes will either add to or subtract from your central message. For example, if you have joined a protest group to curb the building of additional nuclear power plants, you cannot seriously carry out your mission sitting in the rumble seat of a convertible. To stand tall and straight, and often alone, is the best way to have a serious message delivered and received as intended.

9. The successful talker is an intelligent self-critic. You know yourself better than anyone does. If you have practiced as much as you possibly can and talked as sincerely and intelligently as you are capable of, why should you ever feel discouraged? If you read the signals from your audience and felt that they were somewhat negative, what can you do about it? Well, if your listeners were restless and shifting about in their seats, maybe the fault wasn't yours at all. It could have been the late hour, or not enough air in the room, or a thunderstorm outside. If, on the other hand, it was a lovely sunny afternoon with a gentle breeze and the best of all possible conditions for talk, maybe you *can* use some boning up on your communication skills. Perhaps you talked too long or labored over many small points. Maybe you didn't do enough research on your topic. Did you skim over some important supporting evidence? Did your discussion have a beginning, a middle, and an end? Take your cues from your audience. Remember that *everyone* can be reached and made content by your words.

10. The successful talker keeps in mind his ethical responsibilities. The most important ethical responsibility we have as talkers is to be prepared. Once there was a well-known and popular speaker who took a day off to visit and talk with the students of several high schools and colleges. He was supposed to "say a few words" about his profession, which was journalism. At each institution he visited, he arrived late and appeared quite out of breath, as if he had jogged from one place to the next. Many hundreds of eager faces awaited his words with great enthusiasm. Unhappily, when he arrived, winded and disheveled, he had nothing ready for his listeners, nothing at all. He managed to pick a few feeble words out of the air, but his message read: "Ask me if I care." The audience didn't respond at all. They didn't have to. The speaker lost sight of the most important rule of communication: the audience has rights.

CHAPTER II

Nonverbal Talk: You Don't Say

Communication is a two-way street. It includes all the ways by which one mind can affect another. What you don't say is as important as what you do say. You are, after all, more than a "talking head." Every part of your body speaks. All the parts except the mouth speak silently. Whenever you think of the word communication, the use of words comes to mind first. But words often have an incomplete message, which must be finalized or rounded out by a gesture, such as a hug or a handshake. Consider how difficult it would be to tell someone how to execute a new disco dance routine. It is so much easier and clearer to demonstrate the step instead.

Nonverbal talk has to do with the interpretation of symbols given off intentionally or unintentionally by the body. Symbols are signs that stand for something else, in the way that a red traffic light stands for bringing your car to a stop. It is easy to assume that a symbol is clear to everyone because it is perfectly clear to you. For example, what signals do you read as you walk toward other people on a crowded street? Observe groups of people bunched together on a curbstone during lunch hour in a big city. They are waiting for the light to change. What happens next? Two groups, one from each side of the street, start to cross. Both groups somehow manage to land safely on the opposite side. Did they need special instruction in the art of walking in crowds without bumping into each other? Did you ever think why we don't bump into other human beings more than we do? The answer is simple. Without knowing it, we give off signals (symbols) that warn people of our approach. The person coming toward us on a crowded sidewalk interprets our signals in language like this:

Here comes someone straight toward me in my direct path. If she veers ever so slightly to the left, I'll swing my shoulders to the right and we'll miss each other.

Two people on a crash course toward each other think these thoughts, but they do so in the shadow of a split second. Very rarely do we get our signals mixed up. When this happens, it means that one of us interpreted the signals, or the "vibes," inaccurately. Then we wind up doing a kind of two-step to get out of the way again.

The signals you send to other people about your change in bodily direction are both complicated and specific. They come from the eyes, the mouth, the hands, the shoulders, the legs, the sway of the body. The eyes try to find the center of the on-coming person's eyes. They warn him that you are about to move over and make room for two bodies to pass. Even if the other person's eyes avoid yours, there has still been enough time to get the message across. What you are really doing in a fraction of a second is a beautifully mapped out, unrehearsed choreography of the mind. You are, in fact, communicating through body channels to hundreds of strangers who come into your life every day.

Body-Talk

Whether you call the nonwords through which your body communicates body language, kinesics, or nonverbal talk, you are saying that a great many silent messages are sent and received among people. The signals that you emit to others through the vehicle of your body are almost always transmitted in the way that you intend. This is because the body cannot tell a lie. The mouth can lie, when your mind permits it to utter what is false. For example, when you pretend to be having a good time at Aunt Harriet's Thanksgiving dinner, your mouth says one thing and your body says something else. The signals are sent out by your posture, which tends to sag and slump when you are not enjoying yourself. When you are ready to leave, and you say "Thanks. I really had a great time," your body has already said it all. When you say things like "I'm in charge here" with your knees and toes pointed at each other, the body has spoken again. It says "I'm frightened, insecure. I don't want to be here."

In the study of body-speech, be sure to notice signals that others give to you unwittingly. For example, there is quite an art in saying good-bye to someone. Body-talk is used more in the beginning and the end of personal relationships than it is in the middle of them. If you misread certain vital signals that one body sends another, you might make some serious mistakes. Let us briefly consider the various messages that can be transmitted in the act of saying good-bye. The person about to leave may do some or all of the following things:

not look directly at you
become restless; shift about in the chair
open and close a pocketbook or briefcase
shuffle papers, pack them into a neat pile, and fasten them with a
    paper clip
stand up
turn legs and feet toward the door; start taking small steps in the
    direction of the exit
look at watch
cough
nod head mechanically

You should take these signals to mean that someone wants to leave your company. If you want to keep these people as friends or business associates, it is well to pick up their signals and let them go. Misread signals are one of the reasons so many business meetings, discussions, and conversations drag on until everyone is either numb or asleep. Somebody has to say good-bye first. Be alert, too, for people who say things like "We must do this again very soon." Translated, it usually means "Let's take a break from each other for a while. I need space to breathe."

When you host a three-to-five cocktail hour, you can anticipate that there will be someone who won't say good-bye at five o'clock. Is handing one his coat a bit too abrupt? At around five-thirty, most successful talkers would be sure to thank their "dawdling" guest for gracing their party with his presence and inquire if he has transportation home. Body signals, accompanied by the proper word-responses, are usually accurate maps of where and how to go from here. Saying good-bye is only one of the many skills the body knows well.

Body-Walk

You can tell everything you need to know about anyone by their walk. Self-confidence or lack of it shows right through our bones. Our walk tells others how we feel about ourselves. Consider the plight of the tall man who was mugged four times in one year. Consider, too, the frail little old lady who was never bothered when she walked to the stores every day. The tall strong man probably didn't know that the signals his body gave off were: "Take my wallet. I won't protest."

Are You Muggable?

Although he was tall, his walk was hesitant, uneven, unsure. He frequently looked on all sides to check who might be behind him. He clutched his briefcase with both arms crossed in front. He *looked* afraid. The point is, he *expected* to be robbed, so he was.

On the other hand, the little old lady expected nothing of the sort. She walked tall and faced any on-comers with a determined look. She slung her bag resolutely over her shoulder and marched confidently down the street. She did her errands with the anticipated knowledge that this would be a fine day and that she was quite able to exist with minimum effort in a world full of uncertainties. The signals from the little old lady said: "I'm very much in control here. If you disturb me any, you'll be sorry. You see, I'm just not muggable."

Consider for a moment the story of the neurosurgeon. He was a man who looked the part of his profession. He dressed conservatively in nice dark suits. He was clean-cut and just the right middle-age to sport his experience and wisdom. His image was perfect—until he walked. He had a frog gait as if sponges were attached to the soles of his shoes. You might say "Who cares?" Well, his patients did. They thought that his body-walk lacked the alignment a neurosurgeon purports to possess. If his walk conformed to the image of "neurosurgeon" that we have in our heads, it should say to us: "See how perfectly aligned my body is. I can do the same for you."

As for the bus driver who whistles on his job, he tells his passengers, in nontalk, that he is quite a happy man.

Body-Stalk

Arms, legs, head, shoulders, trunk, torso all combine to send out clues to how you think and feel about yourself and the world. Bodies reveal innermost thoughts. They never conceal what we don't want others to know about us. Here is a scene that takes place at a job interview. Observe what goes on nonverbally. See how much the body is capable of communicating on its own, sometimes to our disadvantage.

The reception room is airy and clean. Soft music is playing. One other person is waiting to be interviewed when Fred Fewwords arrives. He is a half hour late. He has just come from a Little League baseball game, which he coaches in his free time. He is dusty and unkempt, but jovial by nature. There is mud on his shoes, and his shoulder-length hair falls in curls over his eyes. The door opens. Mr. B. Sharp, the interviewer, looks around the room and asks who is next. A well-dressed young man in a business suit and tie stands up. Fred, who is obviously in a hurry, asks the other candidate if he can go first because of an important commitment. The interviewer and the candidate agree to Fred's request. The interview begins.

Mr. B. Sharp has already sized up Fred and decided not to hire him because he doesn't like the way Fred looks and acts. He doesn't shake hands because Fred's hands are dirty.

Mr. B. Sharp: Fred, I have a record of your grades here. They don't seem to be too promising for your future.

Translation: You look like you couldn't care less. How dare you come to an interview late and look like an ad for rag-picking. Your school grades are atrocious. You obviously spent a lot of time fooling around.

Fred Fewwords: I know. I had other things to do.

Translation: I could have worked much harder in school, but I had to work three jobs to help out financially at home. My dad is on disability and my younger brothers and sisters really need me around. That's why I donate my spare time to the Little League.

Mr. B. Sharp: I'm sure you had.

Translation: Boy, this guy is a loser. He looks like he's on something and wants this job so he can support his habit.

Fred Fewwords: Mr. Sharp, I'd appreciate it if you could let me know about the job. I have to meet another commitment now.

Translation: I've got to get home, take a shower, and go to night school to make up all those credits I lost while taking care of the family during dad's illness. Hope Mr. Sharp doesn't take this speedy departure in the wrong way.

Mr. B. Sharp: OK, Fred. We'll call you.

Translation: Don't call us. We won't call you. You ran in here late and dashed out before I finished asking questions. You have no respect for authority. Someone ought to buy you a haircut. I can't stand hippies. You'll ruin this country yet.

In the above skit, you can see that the words spoken were not half as important as the words not spoken. If Fred Fewwords had taken care to put himself across as he really is, not as he *appears* to be, he would have gotten the job. After all, he had all the necessary inner qualifications: responsibility, integrity, generosity, ability to work with others. His outer trappings betrayed him. The truth is, you are to others what you appear to be. When you say "Nobody understands me," you really mean that nobody reads your body signals correctly.

You are more than the sum of your separate parts. You bring to your job, your friends, your home, all that you know through exposure, memory, and perception. All your communication channels are selec-

"Adelaide, You Look Divine."

tive. You select only certain experiences from life that are important to you, and you play them hard. If Fred Fewwords had only selected to dress well and be on time, he would have been an obvious winner.

You choose not to expose yourself to every possible human experience because they would take hundreds of years to complete. Instead, you decide which experiences are important for you, and you admit them into your consciousness. You have to turn away many experiences, even valuable ones, because they would crowd your life and not allow you to think.

You also decide to forget certain things in time. Usually these are unpleasant or frightening things or things that held no meaning for you. The expression "Forgive and forget," however, is inaccurate. You can and do forgive, but you file unhappy events away in your memory bank to keep from being hurt again.

Your perceptions color the way you look at things. You are never neutral or indifferent about any person, experience, or object. You see what you have been programmed to see. If Mr. Sharp had not been so closed-minded about long hair, he might have let Fred into the realm of possibility. You tend to categorize everyone you meet so that they slip into convenient boxes in your mind, marked "I accept you," or "I reject you." You react instantly to persons you have just been introduced to or who pass you on the street. In your mind, you affirm or deny their existence with unspoken words like:

I don't think obese people can be very interesting or know much. Her hair is bleached. Blondes are dumb, anyway. She looks dumb. Check the weird hair style on this one. He should grow up. Here comes Mrs. Wildlife. She thinks she's great stuff. I won't speak to her first.

Actions: Louder Than Words

Here is a passage from a witty turn-of-the-century farce by Oscar Wilde, *The Importance of Being Earnest.* The words show the difference between what people say they believe and how they act. The scene shows two young women conversing with words that have meanings opposite to literal translation. Be sure to read the body language in the parentheses.

Cecily (advancing to meet her): Pray, let me introduce myself to you. My name is Cecily Cardew.

Gwendolyn: Cecily Cardew? (Moving to her and shaking hand.) What a sweet name. Something tells me that we are going to be great friends. I like you already more than I can say. My first impressions of people are never wrong.

Cecily: How nice of you to like me so much after we have known each other such a comparatively short time. Pray sit down.

Gwendolyn (still standing up): I may call you Cecily, may I not?

Cecily: With pleasure.

Gwendolyn: And you will always call me Gwendolyn, won't you?

Cecily: If you wish.

Gwendolyn: Then it is all quite settled, is it not?

Cecily: I hope so. (A pause. They both sit down together.)

Gwendolyn: Perhaps this might be a favorable opportunity for my mentioning who I am. My father is Lord Bracknell. You have heard of papa, I suppose?

Cecily: I don't think so.

Gwendolyn: Outside the family circle, papa, I am glad to say, is entirely unknown. . . . Do you mind my looking at you through my glasses?

Cecily: Oh! not at all, Gwendolyn. I am fond of being looked at.

Gwendolyn (after examining Cecily carefully through a lorgnette): You are here on a short visit, I suppose?

Cecily: Oh no! I live here.

Gwendolyn (severely): Really? Your mother, no doubt, or some female relative of advanced years, resides here also?

Cecily: Oh no! I have no mother, nor, in fact, any relations.

Gwendolyn: Indeed?

Cecily: My dear guardian, with the assistance of Miss Prism, has the arduous task of looking after me.

Gwendolyn: Your guardian?

Cecily: Yes, I am Mr. Worthing's ward.

Gwendolyn: Oh! It is strange he never mentioned to me that he had a ward. . . . How secretive of him. . . . (Rising and going to her.) I am very fond of you, Cecily; I have liked you ever since I met you! But I am bound to state now that I know that you are Mr. Worthing's ward, I cannot help expressing a wish you were—well, just a little older than you seem to be—and not quite so very alluring in appearance. In fact, if I may speak candidly—

Cecily: Pray do! I think that whenever one has anything unpleasant to say, one should always be quite candid.

Gwendolyn: Well, to speak with perfect candor, Cecily, I wish that you were fully forty-two, and more than usually plain for your age. Ernest has a strong upright nature. . .

Cecily: I beg your pardon, Gwendolyn, did you say Ernest?

Gwendolyn: Yes.

Cecily: Oh, but it is not Mr. Ernest Worthing who is my guardian. It is his brother—his elder brother.

Gwendolyn (sitting down again): Ernest never mentioned to me that he had a brother.

Cecily: I am sorry to say they have not been on good terms for a long time.

Gwendolyn: Oh! that accounts for it. . . . It would have been terrible if any cloud had come across a friendship like ours, would it not? Of course, you are quite, quite sure that it is not Mr. Ernest Worthing who is your guardian?

Cecily: Quite sure. (A pause.) In fact, I am going to be his.

Gwendolyn (inquiringly): I beg your pardon?

Cecily (rather shy and confidingly): Dearest Gwendolyn, there is no reason why I should make a secret of it to you. Our little country newspaper is sure to chronicle the fact next week. Mr. Ernest Worthing and I are engaged to be married.

Gwendolyn (quite politely, rising): My darling Cecily, I think there must be some slight error. Mr. Ernest Worthing is engaged to me. . . .

Notice how battle is waged through words and gestures. Cecily and Gwendolyn are pretending to be something other than they are. There are many fine examples of affected talk in these passages. Notice the progression of dialogue and nondialogue (gesture) from false friendliness to mild coldness to suspicion and mistrust. As the conversation turns to argument, Gwendolyn finally admits her true feelings for Cecily:

From the moment I saw you I distrusted you. I felt that you were false and deceitful. . . . My first impressions of people are invariably right.

Most of us find it difficult to change our first impressions of others. Education can help to open our minds to perceive new possibilities in people. Personal effort is a tremendous help, too. Remember, there is a way through to everyone. It's all a matter of knowing how.

Space-Walk

How you use the space around you is another aspect of body-talk. Think of the various uses of space that people adjust to. Have you ever tried to listen to someone who was speaking almost on top of your nose? Your first reaction to someone who invades your private circle of space is to take a giant step backward. Of course, there is the great probability that the speaker will take another step forward, forcing you to step back again. Communication of this sort is on dangerous ground. Space is the common commodity that we all carry around with us, along with our bodies and the air they breathe. Space is your inviolate right. You become nervous when someone "steps on your toes." You are tense when your private breathing area is usurped by an unwanted intruder. Usually you need at least one and a half feet between you and another person before any kind of meaningful conversation can take place. If someone closes in on you, your first impulse is to run. You feel pressured and ill at ease.

When you study people's private spaces, you are able to tell as much about them as when you study their words. Observe the following spatial dimensions and see what kind of communication is going on.

You are in the office of Mr. Bert Bigspace, the President of Allied Arts. The room is immense. He has given himself more space than he'll ever need in order to carry out his job functions. When you go to visit him, you stand just inside the door, waiting for him to summon you to the desk area. After ignoring your presence for a while, he finally motions you to approach. He dispenses with common amenities but indicates with a gesture that you should sit down. He does not look at you. The desk is huge, so Mr. Bigspace doesn't reach across it to shake your hand. This tells you much about the man. A warm, communicative human being would stand when a guest enters his private space. He would walk over to you and extend his hand in greeting. Perhaps he might touch your arm or shoulder in a gesture of friendship. He would also be alert to your needs, however, and sense that you might not like to be touched. The person of Bert Bigspace quickly and permanently alienates people. His protection of as much space as he can acquire tells you that he considers himself a superior individual with superior standards. He has neither the time nor the space for ordinary people. Sometimes this type of person is simply a clerk pretending to be king. You can always spot the person of true stature. He treats with kindness and consideration someone who can be of no possible service to him. His space is your space. He can dispense with a desk or other furniture altogether because they create distance between him and his guest. He can exist with a simple chair as long as there is another chair close by for easy access to his friends.

When people talk in a formal situation, they are very conscious of the uses of space. In a classroom situation, you tend to huddle with others for comfort and companionship. When you are asked to "say something," it is more convenient to call out a response from the space around you than to stand or walk to the front of the room. This technique does little to enhance your credibility, however. A response called out from the last row is akin to a lone voice in the wildnerness or a foghorn in a misty harbor. How much better it is to identify yourself and stand if you have a brief remark to make or walk to the front of the room where you can be seen and heard. People react positively to those who believe in their own convictions and opinions.

When you must use a podium to talk, be aware of the special use of space that it provides. You can stand behind it, to the side of it, or in front of it. All these postures mean something different. If you stand directly behind the podium, you convey a formal ambience between you and your hearers. Your arms are usually planted firmly on the sides of the podium, and your script is neatly typed and rehearsed. If you stand to either side of the podium, you present a more relaxed image, confident that you can communicate best in a semicasual way. You can still consult your notes from this angle; they are next to you on the podium, but you don't have to refer to them for every detail. This posture generally encourages some audience interaction. It indicates that the speaker considers himself on friendly, even personal, terms with his listeners. If you choose to stand in front of the podium, it produces the same effect as not having a podium at all. The speaker wants no restraints on his space. He is free to roam into the audience and to converse casually and knowledgeably with his guests. This speaker likes intimacy but doesn't tolerate disorder. He is as well prepared as other, more formal, speakers, but his delivery has the "down home" style, which usually has great appeal. The most informal use of verbal space happens when the talker chooses to sit down during his discussion. This is not the ideal posture for communicating with a large group, however. It says that you don't have the energy needed in order to be dynamic. Also, there is a chance that the audience might yawn and nod off on you if they see only the top of your head. They will miss the flow of your energy. When you stand the universe is your onion.

Another aspect of the use of space in communication is reflected in the design of your home. The placement of furniture at certain intervals or spatial clusters gives definite clues to your personality. For example, what is the physical distance you and a friend occupy when you converse in the living space of your friend's house? If the furniture is grouped in small conversational clusters, your friend has a preference for intimate, personal talk. If, on the other hand, you find a chair and table at one end of a tennis-court living room and a chair and table at the other end, you can guess that your friend is the creator of physical distances. He does not encourage guests to overstay their welcome. In turn, you feel these vibrations and desire to leave at the first possible moment.

Americans have very definite spatial preferences. We walk and talk at greater distances from our friends than do Europeans. We are conscious of defending our private space because we feel we have so little of it. For example, we endure commuter rushes, where we are packed to the touch of one body with another. No wonder we rush to our own cars for some privacy. There is a commercial about the busy mother of five children who seeks a few solitary moments each day in the family station wagon, because there isn't any space to read the newspaper uninterrupted in her house. Americans like to dream of privacy and isolation. That is why travel agencies advertise the "get away from it all" theme.

There are times when you want to relinquish your private space, too. When Yankee Stadium is filled to capacity, you are sitting sardine-close to the persons next to you, and you don't mind at all. You have chosen to share your space with strangers because you are being entertained at a common event. You find that, as spectators, there is a great deal of interaction with the people around you. You cheer and make verbal noises together. You don't miss your lost personal space. You need other bodies around you in order to make your enthusiasm felt.

Personal spaces vary within cultures. Some cultures encourage the men to converse with arms around each other's shoulders, as in a mild embrace. We frown on such customs, thinking it too personal a stance. Some Far Eastern countries expect the women to walk down the street holding hands with each other. We would frown on that practice, too, and give it an unpopular label.

Time: Short-Stop

It has been said that character is the product of mental attitude and the way we spend our time. You need time to communicate well, time to build and strengthen personal relationships. Statements like "If only I had the time," and "There aren't enough hours in the day," are common complaints. Of course there are enough hours in any day to do what you must get done. It's all a matter of organizing your priorities. The most successful people can deal with the clock as if it were a good friend. Time is a fine hidden communicator.

In our culture the successful person is one who doesn't keep others waiting. If a meeting is scheduled for ten o'clock in the morning, the word "sharp" should be imprinted on the mind. All of us know certain types who are habitually late. Sometimes we think of them as "arty" folk, who have not the slightest intention of following a scheduled pattern. If you invite some habitual latecomers to your home for dinner, you usually tell the prompt guests to come at seven o'clock and the "late arrivals" to come at six. In that way, everybody can be expected at seven.

Time, as a means of communication, is vital to your personality. People who are punctual are also likely to be listened to when they talk. They are not likely to waste other people's time in frivolous conversation or gossip. They don't dawdle. They are aware of the passage of time and doubly aware of its potential in their lives. Time propels you to the right contacts and the right places. It enables you to move ahead each hour with the certainty that you are experiencing new, valuable things.

There was a young man who was very talented as a landscape painter. A prospective employer agreed to interview him at one o'clock on a certain day. The young artist promised to be there, but on his way to the interview he met a friend who invited him to lunch. The sidewalk cafe was only a block from the employer's office. The artist was oblivious to the passage of time and enjoyed a leisurely lunch until two o'clock. The employer arrived at the same cafe at two o'clock for a late lunch. Seeing the artist, he reminded him of their appointment, but the artist appeared indifferent to the commitment. Time had communicated more than words to the employer. Anyone in the business of communicating— and that's just about everyone—has to understand that it is nearly impossible to beat the system. You can't work outside the structure and maintain credibility. Although working within it may not be easy all the time, it provides the only conceivable means of calling yourself a success. If my time is not your time, then we had better get together and agree on a common clock that summons us both. Who knows how many channels of communication have been shut down because someone has been "stood up"? Your trusty watch may be your best nonverbal communicator.

Included in the concept of time is the use of silence. This is the short-stop that refreshes your words. Because you are preoccupied with not wasting time, your speech is usually too rapid for the best possible impact. You can always remind yourself to slow down, but the effect is temporary. You can send secret signals to yourself, like a quick pinch on the elbow, but you naturally want to speed up again and get it over with. Time is of the essence, you feel, and you don't want to risk boredom on the part of your listeners.

In order to be a successful talker, you must get used to living with silences. These pauses are wonderful little spaces of rest in the middle or at the end of your thoughts. They let you spend time without wasting it. Silences are nonverbal cues to your hearers that give them time to absorb what you are saying. Silences are absolutely necessary for talk to be good. You can learn to live with them very handily by doing a few exercises.

An easy way to put on the verbal brakes is to glance over your manuscript and draw a circle around the final consonant of each word. Here is a sample sentence:

He carries his self-importance as if he were afraid
that it might break.

If that sentence were in your script, you might be tempted to say it this way:

Hecarrieshisself-importanceasifhewereafraidthatitmightbreak.

When you mark up your script with a brightly colored Flair pen, your notes might read:

He carrie⑤ hi⑤ sel⑥-importance a⑤ i⑥ he were afrai⑥ tha① i① migh① brea⑥.

Let your eye come to rest on the circles at the end of the final-consonant words. It will automatically slow down the flow of words from your mouth. This method requires some time and effort, but it is well worth it when people say that they enjoy listening to you. Don't be afraid to take the audience's time when you talk. After all, they wouldn't be listening to you in the first place if they didn't think well of you.

When mapping out your pause-time or stops, be sure that the main ideas in your talk are carried out as you intend. There can only be one main idea each time you say something.

Another silence to remember is the five-second pause just before you begin to talk and immediately after you have concluded. This "comma" in your body language gives the extra polish that makes you more professional. Five seconds may seem like an eternity to you, but it is hardly noticed by your hearers. It is a subtle way of letting everyone know that you are in command and that you know what you are about to say, even if you feel unsure. The body communicates essential vibrations before you begin to talk. In fact, a thoroughly unprofessional talker might forget to control his nerves by deep breathing. He might, in panic, dash up to the front of the room and start the words flowing while he is en route. Similarly, when he sees from his notes that he is almost finished, he is so overjoyed that he prepares to dart back to the safety of his chair before the conclusion has been spoken. When you talk, the time needed to achieve a polished beginning and a well-rounded conclusion is about ten seconds. While you are calming yourself appropriately in this time, be sure to use those vital seconds to fix your eyes on your hearers. Sweep your gaze around the room at least once, like a movie-camera lens, and fasten upon as many pair of eyes as you can find. If your group is small enough, say eight or fewer, this act of solidarity shouldn't be difficult to perform.

"Cool" Aids

One of the current meanings of "cool" is "pleasing" or "very nice." An aid, of course, is something that helps you to do something else in a more efficient way. Aids in speech are usually nonverbal, active, visual props that help to put your message across. Here are some of the most common aids with their most common uses:

The blackboard. This old-fashioned device can be very supportive to your discussion or presentation. If you should ever decide to use one, there are a few tricks to remember. For one, be sure not to turn your back to your listeners. The temptation to face the chalkboard head-on when writing on it can be quite strong. If your listeners have to look at your back for any length of time, you risk losing them. Once they have been distracted from you for even a few seconds, it is almost impossible to win them back. A second point to remember when you use the blackboard is that you don't have to be an art major or an illustrator for *Vogue* in order to push your message along. What is needed is a design that is both quick and simple. For example, if you are talking to the local garden society about raising a certain kind of flower or leaf, sketch it roughly in outline form. Talk and draw at the same time. Never address your words to the board. Practice as much as you can until the blackboard presentation *appears* effortless and easy.

The sketch pad on easel. The skill involved in this kind of presentation

Mr. A-V

is the same as that needed for the blackboard talk, but there is a definite advantage to using pencil or ink drawings on the sketch pad. These can be done before you begin your talk, and you know how they will turn out. You can flip the pages over as your discussion proceeds. Your outline will tell you when to turn the page. This type of talk requires the use of both hands, so you can expect to be busy. You will need to be turning the pages of the sketch pad and flipping through your notes on index cards at the same time. You might feel more comfortable with a podium on one side of you and the sketch pad on the other. This is an excellent way to present difficult material or to illustrate simple ideas in a powerful, impressive way.

The graph. Several kinds of graphs are available for use in a serious discussion. The bar graph gives a relationship to sets of figures. The line graph shows two or more variable facts or figures in concert with each other. Picture graphs show amounts or degrees of growth by the number and size of the symbols.

The enlarged picture or photograph. A good picture can have the impact of many words, but the picture alone is worthless to your discussion. You must supply background or foreground information to set the central theme. The illustration should be introduced as the clincher to your argument. Be sure that it has been enlarged. With a standard size picture, the audience would be straining to see it, and they would lose you in the process. Don't pass around your illustration. By the time it travels the room, members of your group have lost you at different times while looking at the picture.

The flannel or felt board. This is a large piece of flannel or felt pulled tightly across and anchored securely behind an ordinary flat board. Cutouts are used to illustrate ideas, facts, or concepts. The cutouts, made from the same flannel material, adhere quickly to the board when you press them on. Be sure to tilt the board slightly, however. If it is perfectly vertical, the cutouts will slide off. Use sharply contrasting colors, such as yellow on a black backdrop, to get your message across.

The object you are talking about. If, for example, you sell fishing tackle, it would make sense to have a box of various devices rather than draw each one on the blackboard or make cutouts for the flannel board. It would be helpful to have as many samples of tackle as there are people listening to you. In this way, they may also get to touch and feel the object.

The model. Models are scaled-down or scaled-up replicas of the object of your discussion. They are useful when you are talking in great detail about intricate material. Models can be cut away to show the inner components of the structure. For example, the owner of a new Holiday Inn might want to show a model of it—that is, a Holiday Inn in miniature—to civic groups that might be interested in using the facility.

The handout. This is usually typed, photocopied, or mimeographed material used to supply additional information beyond the speaker's scope of the subject. Such documents can reinforce the speaker's message when his talk has concluded. The audience has something to take home to refresh their memory. It is best for the speaker to distribute handouts after the presentation unless he or she wants the group to join in an item-by-item discussion. Audiences tend to be easily distracted; if you put papers in their hands, they will read them.

The film, slide, or tape. These are helpful if used sparingly. You need only a small portion of a film, slide, or tape to illustrate your main idea forcefully. Anything more than that allows the audience to forget about you and imagine that they are relaxing in a theater.

Other people as demonstrators of your idea. This is occasionally useful if your presentation requires a demonstration to clarify the main point. If, for example, you are arguing for mandatory karate lessons as part of the high-school curriculum, a demonstration lesson by a karate expert would serve to support your proposed program of self-defense. If you find yourself explaining to a small group the basic steps of ballet, bring along a six-year-old to show how easy it really is.

Any of the above aids, if used correctly, can serve to enhance your words. The key to the success of visual supports is that they are second in importance to the speaker and should never be given free rein in a talk. The use of visuals requires even more practice than a straight talk would, because the speaker has to know exactly when, where, and how long his aids must perform. He must be careful to control them, or they will control him.

Is Anybody Listening?

It is the disease of not listening, the malady of not marking, that I am troubled with.

—Shakespeare

Popular songwriters Paul Simon and Art Garfunkel once wrote a message-tune that had to do with people hearing without listening. Listening is perhaps the most important kind of nonverbal communication. It is the active involvement and participation in the total message of another. Hearing, on the other hand, is simply the involuntary absorption of sound as it is received by the ear. Most of us listen some of the time to some of a message. Consequently, there are gaps in the apprehension of true meanings. For example, there is the story of the politician who went about the countryside campaigning for "a chicken in every pot and two cars in every garage." What with the crowds and the noise factor and the microphones clicking on and off, his message sounded more like "a chicken, a pot, and some cars." To be a careful listener is an art all its own. After a while, good listeners really begin to know something. You don't have to be talking all day in order to be popular. Listeners are much more in demand than talkers. If you listen well, wonderful things can happen to you. No one has ever been known to listen himself out of a job.

The following story on the effects of poor listening serves to illustrate the point.

A message was given by a colonel to a major: "At nine o'clock tomorrow morning I am conducting a full inspection of this camp. Have all the men in dress uniforms, with their rifles cleaned and barracks shipshape. Let there be no mistake."

The major communicated the message immediately to the captain: "The colonel, at nine o'clock tomorrow morning, is conducting an inspection while dressed. Have the men wear clean uniforms and leave the rifles by mistake in shipshape barracks."

The captain to the lieutenant: "The colonel will be dressed for inspection by nine o'clock tomorrow morning. He will wear a clean uniform which was shippped by mistake with the rifles to the shipshape barracks."

The lieutenant communicated clearly to the sergeant: "The colonel will be shipped by mistake to the rifle barracks at nine o'clock tomorrow morning, where he will conduct an inspection of clean dress uniforms."

The sergeant then confided to the corporal: "At nine o'clock tomorrow morning the mistaken colonel, with clean rifle, will inspect the dresses to be shipped from the barracks."

Finally, private to private: "The old guy has flipped. I heard he's being shipped out for planning to wear a clean dress and rifle for inspection tomorrow at nine o'clock in the barracks. There must be some mistake."

While this banter might seem farfetched as a lesson in listening, it is not entirely off-base. You frequently hear only small parts of messages, and so you confuse the main idea with some of the detail. You can easily make the mistake of hearing what you want to hear.

In order to be an effective listener, ask yourself some key questions:

1. Do you "get ready" to listen? That is, do you enter the room of the speaker with a positive attitude? If possible, try to like the speaker *before* he or she arrives. Listening requires an active, forward thrust. You have to be consciously in the mood to listen.

2. Do you feel that, however poor the speaker might be, you can still come away knowing more than you did before you entered the room? If you answered "yes" to this question, you will make every experience an opportunity for personal growth. You will feel that there is so much to learn and you can't know less than you did yesterday.

3. Do you listen especially to catch the central idea of the speaker? Speakers, even indifferent ones, can only talk about one thing at a time. What the speaker says primarily or emphatically is the main idea.

4. Do you tune in to only the light or humorous parts of a talk? Remember that the jokes are only there to get your attention. They are not what the talk is *about*. Jokes are attacks on our passivity. They may relieve boredom for the moment, but they leave us empty.

5. Do you watch the mannerisms of the speaker, his gestures, his white socks, his plaid tie with the striped shirt? Most talkers have pet gestures of the hand, or some favorite expression that keeps cropping up during the presentation. For example, Winston Churchill gave us the popular "victory sign," which President Richard M. Nixon made less popular. Many speakers have a proliferation of awkward expressions like "Y'know what I mean?" One can easily overdo these personal idiosyncrasies. The audience will be sure to count the times a favorite mannerism or expression is used.

6. Why do you half-listen? If it is because you are sincerely not interested in what is being said, then you either (a) shouldn't have attended this meeting, or (b) hoped that a bright, new, wonderful approach to the subject by a dynamic, sensitive talker would cause you to become interested. There isn't any subject that is entirely uninteresting. If you met the right talker on the subject you like least, you would be converted instantly.

7. Do you "un-listen" because you don't want to believe what the speaker is saying? This sometimes happens when a speaker talks about an idea or a concept that is opposite to your own view. For instance,

politicians not of our persuasion don't get our full ear because we know in advance that we are not going to agree.

8. Do you refrain from listening because you don't like the speaker? If this is so, why, exactly, don't you like the speaker? Is it personality? Dress? Is it because a friend or a distant cousin told you that he is "all fluff and no stuff"? Remember, anyone who stands before a group of any size takes a giant leap of faith. It takes courage to open your mouth and talk. The speaker is *always* fearful that his hearers won't like him. He tries even harder to please an alien group than to please his friends.

9. Contrarily, do you listen attentively and purposefully because you like the speaker a lot? Perhaps he was your speech coach in junior high and you think he is just adorable. But why listen in a state of pious coma? He may not, after all, be making that much sense. Listen for *ideas* and how they hang together. If they are poorly expressed, even the brightest personality won't help.

10. Do your emotions keep you from listening at your best capacity? Can you be so intense over an issue that you cannot bring yourself to hear the other side of the argument? Here the fine line is drawn between the educated, open-minded person who makes decisions based on fact, and the emotionally swayed, opinion-oriented person who goes with the crowd.

Why bother to listen at all? For survival, to be sure. The life of body and soul hang on the thread of information that is dispensed to us daily. There are several types of listening available to us. We can listen to be entertained. Who of us has not enjoyed the fast one-liners of Neil Simon's comedies? You have only to listen to the surface meaning of *The Odd Couple* to be tickled into submission. This kind of listening is good more for the spirit than for the mind. It is what we call easy listening, because it doesn't require a commitment or a conviction. It just requires our tired selves after a long day's work. Monty Python or Bob Hope or any of the situation comedies on television will serve the purpose of surface entertainment. If they didn't satisfy the need we have to relax utterly, we wouldn't have listened so long and so well to Archie's "Bunkerisms" over the years.

We listen in order to escape from the pressures and tensions of every-day life. Sports, television police shows, fast-action thrillers, and even catastrophe films fall under this heading. We are transported to another world. Who cares about the realm of possibility when we're making an escape?

The next type of listening is listening for inspiration. This type implies a more conscious effort on our part. We need inspiration for survival, so we set out to find it in our churches, clubs, and friends. Listen to the coach who gives his team a pep talk before the big game. The team needs his words in order to win. People like Knute Rockne and General George Patton were especially able to move tired bodies to victory. Their words had to be listened to as well as heard. Inspiration is diffused to us from pulpits, from the lips of great leaders, from people we know who have transcended great obstacles in order to live and be ennobled by their experiences.

When you set out deliberately to learn something, you listen for information and ideas. This is the kind of listening that is supposed to go on in classrooms. It implies more than note-taking, however. To listen well, in this category, you should listen for *essences,* that is, for those ideas that are paramount in a lecture or discussion. On that subject, the taking down of every word as a pearl of wisdom to be cherished doesn't mean a thing in the improvement of listening skills. It simply points to the fact that you can't distinguish the important from the filler. Every speaker has a central message with a few subsidiary ones. All else is embellishment. A good talker repeats the central theme in several ways.

Information and ideas come to us from politicians and newsmakers, from professional people and writers of foreign and domestic policy. They come from poets and artists, clergymen and craftsmen. We need to know what they say in order to survive. For example, you have to know the duration and intensity of the gasoline shortage because such knowledge will directly affect your vocational plans.

You listen to evaluate and arrive at decisions. You mull over what you read in the newspaper. You consider, you weigh, you evaluate all the information that comes at your senses in large daily doses. You cannot possibly do this well until you have learned to listen productively.

Your decisions in life, major or minor, hang in the balance of your good judgment.

Here are some hints to help you to listen more efficiently:

1. Ask yourself what is the single most important idea in the message you just heard. How many parts or sections were there in that message? What specific phrases or gestures did the speaker employ to drive home his main point? Did the loudness of his voice signify that he was saying something more important than a softer voice would imply? Could he wipe you out with a whisper? Voice tone is important in the deciphering of meanings.

2. Make a mental note of all the examples the speaker used to support his main idea.

3. Try to remember the exact words that opened and closed the talk.

4. Look for specific organizational patterns in the remarks. Observe how the speaker moved from one idea to another. Try to remember the words he used to make the transitional leaps.

Listening as an art form requires a constant, steady observation of the detail of daily life. Memory is the key to listening in a grand manner. To help you to cultivate this skill, have a friend name a dozen well-known celebrities. See if you can recall all the names. First try to categorize them in their specific fields. For example, Johnny Carson would fit in the "talk-show-host" slot. Archie Bunker goes under the "sitcom" heading.

Listen to a grocery list. Try to recall all the items without writing them down. Allow the list to become longer each time you play this game. A good memory is a valuable asset to the successful talker. Memories are cultivated. They don't happen automatically.

Another good listening exercise is to tell a third person what you understand a speaker to have said. Do this as soon as a speaker concludes. Never let a speaker go until you have understood his points thoroughly. When in doubt, ask questions. It shows that you care about what is being said.

To further heighten your powers of listening, you have to do a great deal of looking. The eye is, after all, the passage to the ear. Look at highway signs and ask yourself if they are clear in meaning. What color are they? When were the old yellow and black signs replaced with the green and white ones? If a sign reads "Schools: Go slow," it can be *heard* as "Schools go slow." What about the sign that reads "merge"? Merge with what? When? Who cares? Everyone sees a "Bump" warning now and then. Often there is no bump at all, or a very minor one, after you anticipate a huge elevation in the road.

In sum, listening can be used for fun and profit. You can listen your way to success if you follow the simple plans set down in these pages. In addition, you can always place yourself in a location where you can listen more accurately. Be sure to find a seat that helps you to see and listen best. If you hug the last chair in the last row you'll be poking your neck around everyone's shoulders for a view of the talkers. Also, sitting in a slump or "hammock" posture turns your mind cloudy and makes your body numb. See if you can meet the eyes of talkers as often as possible. When eyes join in a common vision, sparks of understanding fill the air waves between.

The art of listening can be learned. Most of us are poor listeners, but we become better with practice. You should be able to distinguish fact from opinion in the same way that you accept or reject the sales pitch of your local used-car dealer. Keep and use only the good ideas from others' words. Be sure that when you listen, you share the same set of language symbols used by the speaker. For example, national audiences who saw Woody Allen's film *Manhattan* generally agreed that you had to live in New York in order to understand the experience.

Clothes-Line

What you wear speaks quite candidly about what you are really like inside. You would scarcely participate in a sailboat race wearing formal dinner clothes. Clothes are extensions of yourself. They reveal where you have been and where you want to go. The world of dress is a world of images and symbols. In a sense, clothes are costumes you put on in order to audition for the roles you want. Clothing is a strong communicator. It heralds your personal and professional identity as soon as you walk into a room. All clothing is a uniform of sorts. Surgeons and scientists can be spotted by their white coats. A judge wearing a flowing white wig creates an image of his own. The academic garb of cap and gown broadcasts a story of personal achievement to strangers who witness a commencement program. All of us like to look a little like everyone else. We think of unity when we think "uniform." We also think of conformity. Blue jeans are the uniform of

You Label Yourself by What You Wear.

the masses, but they don't tax the imagination or offer the challenge to come up with something different.

Nobody likes to be out of step when it comes to clothing. The hippies of the 1960's had their own special clothing code. It had a language all its own. For the hippie cult, long hair, beards, bare feet, "ventilated" jeans, assorted neck beads, and gray-white undershirts *with* sleeves announced the following message to the blue- and white-collar workers of middle America:

We don't like the way you turned out.
Who needs money to survive?

Friendship and free sunny days are all any of us need.

You're a slave to the system. You'll probably die of ulcers and heart attacks.

You don't know the meaning of life.

To the hippie community, the blue- and white-collar workers of middle America responded in kind:

We don't like the way you turned out.

You *do* need money to survive. It's nice to work for it.

Friendship and free time are nice on your annual two-week vacation. You've got to be going *somewhere,* or you'll take several steps backward.

This country was built out of a passionate desire to see things improve. We're always looking for the better way.

You don't know the meaning of life.

When you wear certain kinds of clothing you communicate your inner state of mind and well-being. Why have a dress code that leaves you anonymous? Why serve a corporate image when your own image is so exciting? Your attire announces your presence in a room before you open your mouth. Your first appearance is your clothing. Your second appearance is your speech. You can cancel yourself if you go to dangerous extremes with either one. Be aware that clothing also includes tattoos, hair dye, makeup, jewelry, slogans printed on T-shirts. Taking the middle road is a good idea for one just starting out in a company on a new job. Wait and see what kind of clothing is appreciated at work. When in doubt, be tailored and conservative in style and color.

The Magic Touch

The last of the nonverbal communicators we will discuss is that of touching. Sometimes you hear the expression "Don't touch me!" from someone who moves away at the possibility of human flesh colliding in some small way. The language of touch is the most earthy of our communicators. It is a language we share with animals and flowers alike.

Observe all the possible ways to communicate by touch. Touch is the first language of newborns. Cubs cling to their mothers without wanting to break touch. To be entirely alone in the world, with no one to reach out to and touch, is a devastating experience for babies of all kinds. Observe an infant who is a few days old. He is already touching everything in sight, even though his own sight is a bit dim. He touches his hands, his feet, his own limited surroundings. He'd like to touch everything beyond those surroundings, too.

Through advanced research, psychologists are able to tell us with certainty that the infant who is touched a lot, bounced, roughed up playfully, tickled, hugged, carried around on people's shoulders, is likely to become a balanced, contented adult. We carry the need for tactile communication—that is, touch—throughout our lives. Look at the language of touch in each of these instances:

> a pat on the head of an injured child, along with soft-spoken words of assurance.
> lovers walking in lockstep, arm in arm in a world that was made for them.
> the need to touch without words during a time of sorrow.
> soldiers embracing loved ones on their return from the war zone.
> the caresses of a small child and his new puppy.
> two little friends holding hands.

With so much importance attached to touch as a means of communicating, it is no wonder that the simple act of handshaking is not simple at all. The handshake is usually the first physical signal of friendship after meeting someone. Don't underestimate its importance. If you grip another's hand in a shallow, flabby, or weak manner and avert your eyes from his at the same time, the combination of effects can be deadly. The handshake should be firm and generous, but not held too long or it becomes a comic gesture.

Here are a few projects to heighten your awareness of nonverbal talk:

1. Stand facing someone and carry on a simple dialogue. Experiment with various spatial distances from each other. Start with a distance that feels normal for you. Next, repeat the same dialogue, or one like it, standing closer together. How do the different distances affect your communication?

2. Choose a television personality who plays his or her own self and imagine what he or she would be like if a complete change of style in dress were required. For example, imagine Marie Osmond wearing Cher's slinky, dazzling gowns, or Johnny Carson going Liberace-style.

3. Give a talk of about three minutes in length standing as close to your listeners as possible. Repeat your words, standing as far away as you can from the group. What difference did the physical distance make? Repeat the talk once again while sitting down. How did this posture affect your reception?

4. Study nonverbal communication on the streets. How do people defend their private spaces?

5. Observe nonverbal signals in a crowded elevator. How many people consult their watch or tap nervously on the floor? How many stare straight ahead and avoid eye contact? Be especially perceptive of those who were conversing with each other in the lobby before the elevator arrived. Did they continue to talk once they were within the confines of the moving elevator? Chances are they didn't, because their private spaces had been strained in the closeness of the elevator.

6. Try to give directions to someone's house nonverbally; that is, without the use of words. Use pictures, diagrams, maps.

7. Practice recalling all the details, in sequential order, of a familiar fairy tale or nursery rhyme. For a different twist, tell your story from the viewpoint of the wolf in "Little Red Riding Hood," or from Sneezy's view in "Snow White and the Seven Dwarfs."

8. Using only the language of touch, instruct a partner to move around the room in the direction in which you steer him or her.

9. Give a talk while the audience turns their backs on you. How does this body-talk affect your enthusiasm and delivery?

10. "Eavesdrop" on several conversations and note the listening traits of each partner. Check eye-touch, body-touch, rigidity, or relaxation.

CHAPTER III

Polishing the Gem

This chapter will discuss making better use of the talk skills that you already have. If you are looking to challenge yourself, you can use your speech to climb the ladder of success. After all, if you can mumble efficiently, the next step to clear and distinct speech isn't that far away. All you need is some practice, the friendship of people who believe in you, and your belief in yourself.

Outwitting the Monotone

A person with a monotone type of voice rarely captures his listeners, or even one listener. A monotone voice can be spotted on an imaginary cardiograph printout. When the graph reads a straight line, you know you're in trouble. Consider what the Dallas Cowboys Cheerleaders would sound like if all their cheers were emitted on a single high-pitched note. What if the collegiate "Rah-rah" cheer were uttered in an inaudible whisper? When someone asks "How are you?" you can tell by the bend in the voice, or the inflection, if that person really cares how you are. Inflection is the word used to refer to the change of pitch within a syllable or word. Its companion, intonation, has to do with the rise and fall of the voice throughout the breath-group or phrase. For example, the standard high-school cheer

Two, four, six, eight
Who do we appreciate?

has universally known inflections and intonations. When you consider that few of us went to the same high school but everyone knows the cheer, it is probable that many of our communication patterns arise from cultural bonds that are instinctively preserved. The same would

"And in Conclusion, I Leave the Bulk of My $2 Billion Estate to . . ."

be true of specialized chants of native tribes in less developed cultures. Patterns of voice "catch on" and are passed from one generation to another intact.

Here are some sentences to practice with for better talk-appeal. The following commands and simple statements usually have downward glides or intonations:

This is the end.
Turn around.
I am leaving now.
Go away.
Do it now.

When you ask a question that can be answered with a simple "yes" or "no," you usually give it an upward glide.

Do you really think so?
Do you mean it?

Wasn't that great?
Will you wash the car?
Isn't that wonderful?

If you ask a question that calls for a statement as an answer, and not a simple "yes" or "no," you frequently use a downward intonation.

Where are you going?
What did I tell you?
Who is that?
What time is it?
Why didn't you say something?

Here, what you are doing to the voice is adding more melody. When Jackie Gleason says "And away we go!" we can anticipate the melody because so many people are familiar with it. Melody is the harmony in our wind instrument, the voice. It is concerned with the movement of the voice up and down the scale. It accounts for appropriate changes in pitch in order to express various meanings and feelings. Take the short sentence, "I'm sorry." Say it in several ways to suggest different meanings.

I'm sorry. (Really I am. That was a stupid thing for me to do.)
I'm sorry. (Said by the man at the box office who has run out of
            tickets for tonight's performance.)
I'm sorry. (I stepped on your toe.)
I'm sorry. (Wrong number.)
I'm sorry. (Illness of a dear friend.)

Here is a full-length selection from a famous scripture passage. The passage can be used to exercise the bending of your voice. The sign (↗) indicates a rising inflection. The sign (↘) indicates a falling inflection. The words underlined are to be emphasized. The asterisks (*) and (**) indicate the short and long pause respectively.

Though I <u>speak</u> with the tongues of <u>men</u> and of <u>angels</u>, * and have not charity, * I am become as sounding brass, or a tinkling cymbal.

* And though I have the gift of prophecy, * and understand all

mysteries, and all knowledge; * and though I have all faith, * so

that I could remove mountains, * and have not charity ** I am

nothing. * And though I bestow all my goods to feed the poor, *

and though I give my body to be burned, * and have not charity,

** it profiteth me nothing. * Charity suffereth long and is kind; *

charity envieth not; * charity vaunteth not itself; is not puffed up;

doth not behave itself unseemly; * seeketh not its own; is not easily

provoked, * thinketh no evil; * rejoiceth not in iniquity, * but rejoiceth

in the truth; ** beareth all things, believeth all things, hopeth all

things, endureth all things **.

Talking Easy

The last line in *Cool Hand Luke,* a film starring Paul Newman, is:
"What we have here is a failure to communicate." The last words of
a similar film, *Easy Rider,* are "We blew it." For ourselves, if we have
too many failures in communicating, we will surely "blow it," that
is, our future. Talking should be an easy and natural process. If we
want to be listened to with enthusiasm, there are some areas in talk
that we all need to improve. Let's call these areas the five P's.
The first things to do when you know you must talk seriously are
these:

Poke about for source material. This is also known as "casing the place." When doing this, don't forget about *you* as a primary source for what you can say. To remind you how much you already know, imagine yourself suddenly transplanted to a foreign country. All the natives are sitting around you asking questions about what life is like in America: the gas shortage, your pet peeve, why you have to spend half your life in school, and so on. You would be able to talk nonstop for several hours and have plenty left to say.

It's Hard to Work Outside the System.

Other people are good sources for your talk stockpile. People whom you respect and are friends with will talk freely about their ideas, opinions, and convictions. It is a good idea to have many "key" friends in many "key" places. Then you have ready access to what they know and are willing to share with you. Also, such friendships keep the lines of communication open for future reference. Newspeople do this. Every person they meet is a potential friend. When it comes to moving ahead in life, you can't have too many friends.

Books, newspapers, and magazines need to be read some part of each day if you really want to stay on top of things. The successful talker always has something worthwhile to say. He knows that his scope needs to be larger than himself and his own life. Listeners tire of "I" talk. To go beyond yourself is a sign of the forward look, a key to advancement at any level.

Movies, radio, and television also require your constant attention. The successful talker knows what shows will give information that might help him on his way to the top. Remember, your image is enhanced by the programs you refuse to watch as well as by those you never miss. For example, a steady diet of catastrophe films featuring earthquakes, man-eating sharks, and towering infernos will hardly serve to round out your personality.

Travel is always a wonderful source for what you know. If you can't travel far and wide, travel locally. Walk in your own neighborhood as if it were a foreign country. Pretend that you are a tour guide. What would you tell a crowded bus of tourists about this block, this town, this state? Be sure to observe everything on your walking tour. Notice when a building gets a "new look," or a whole block starts to shape up. Take a bus tour to the end of the line, and make the return trip on another bus line or a train.

Sources for your knowledge are all around you. Use them wisely and well.

Prepare to talk. Always be in a state of proximate preparedness. Take some part of every day to rehearse, just as a professional athlete does, for the time when you can talk well when it matters most to your career. Constant readiness is a great idea. It demands that you know a lot about yourself in order to tone up weak spots. For example, if you know that you talk too fast, take time on otherwise quiet days to do some exercises on slowing down. One suggestion is to take words apart, that is, chop them up into syllables and say them in their "syllabled" form. This will automatically put the voice-brakes on for you. Below is a sample of this kind of exercise.

His' to-ry, with its mys' ter-y of my-thol' o-gy and bois' ter-ous vic' to-ries, is gen' er-al-ly more in'ter-est-ing than the ac' cu-rate work of a-rith' me-tic and ge-om' e-try. Hy' giene, too, and sev' er-al other sub' jects are quite as val' u-a-ble, my guar' dian says, as al ge-bra and ge-og' raphy.

This may not make much sense as literature, but it does make you deal more particularly with sounds within words.

If you don't know how to pronounce certain words, don't hesitate to look up their meaning and pronunciation. Everyone has a private list of words about which he or she isn't clear. The trouble in pronouncing certain words may stem all the way back to childhood. Tackle them now, and your future will be brighter. The truth of the world out there is that we *do* have to impress people who can do things for us. Talking is such a powerful statement of self that it warrants our closest attention for the greatest development. Remember, we serve ourselves when we serve our speech.

Some Common Errors in Pronunciation

across—do not add a "t"

alms—the "l" is silent

asked—don't drop the "k"

balk and balm—the "l" is silent

battle—cut the "t" clearly

blithe—rhyme with scythe

cache—rhyme with rash

calm and chalk—the "l" is silent

chef—"ch" has the sound of "sh"

chic—rhymes with sheik

chute—pronounced "shoot"

clothes—do not say "close"

data—do not say "dada"

drowned—rhyme with found

elm—one syllable

era—first syllable "e" as in "eve"; the "r" goes with the "a"

extra—avoid "tree"

film—one syllable

friend—don't drop the "d"

gesture—"g" as in gem

golf—pronounce the "l"

heir—silent "h"

kept—say the final "t"

most—say the "t"

often—say "offen"

palm—silent "l"

poem—two syllables

probably—three syllables

psalm, qualm—the "l" is silent

regular—pronounce "u" as in unite

remember—say the first syllable

riding—do not say "writing"

sandwich—last syllable is "witch"

softly—do not drop the "t"

sophomore—three syllables

subtle—silent "b"

suppose—do not drop the "u"

sword—drop the "w"; rhyme with cord

toward—drop the "w"

Tuesday—first syllable rhymes with "fuse"

twenty—pronounce both "t's"
Wednesday—first syllable rhymes
   with "lens"
whoop—drop the "w"; rhymes
   with stoop

worst—don't drop the "t"
writhe—"w" is silent; rhymes with
   scythe
zero—rhyme first syllable with
   "ear"

Talking too slowly is a rare condition. It may mean that you just can't get started, or when you do you feel that what you say doesn't really matter. You come to a near halt, lowering your volume as well as your eyes. These signals tell of your lack of trust in yourself. You have, in truth, many wonderful things to say, and anyone worth his salt should be delighted to hear you. Here are a few lines to help speed up your adrenalin and let those abundant juices flow. They are from Robert Browning's poem "The Pied Piper of Hamelin."

And out of the houses the rats came tumbling
Great rats, small rats, lean rats, brawny rats,
Brown rats, black rats, gray rats, tawny rats
Grave old plodders, gay young friskers
Fathers, mothers, uncles, cousins
Cocking tails and pricking whiskers
Families by the tens and dozens
Brothers, sisters, husbands, wives—
Followed the piper for their lives.

While you are preparing to talk more effectively and efficiently, don't skimp on the task of sharpening your words. This project is called improving diction. It implies the cutting of each word sharply so that the full sound is heard in its entirety. Everybody needs these practices. They are vital to the life of good talk. We all speak sloppily from time to time, as we all dress sloppily on occasion. We know that we're in trouble when people ask us to repeat what we are saying. If our words sound like this:

"Hey, Pete, any guy wot says 'tomāto,' instead of
'tomäto' is nuttin but a uncout bum,"

we should run, not walk, to the nearest set of diction exercises. When our conversation consistently runs the gamut of lip-lazy language, we hear mutilated phrases of this sort:

"Hey, jeet?" (Did you eat?)
"No, jew?" (No, did you?)
"He wuz aweez sayin sumpin like we hafta tell da troot."
(He was always saying something like we have to tell the truth.)

You almost need an interpreter for language of this sort. Because the chiseling of words is so critical to their meaning, you should prepare yourself for practice exercises by doing some deep-breathing calisthenics. Here are a few.

Stand comfortably but not rigidly. The chest is active. One foot is slightly in advance of the other to maintain balance. Let the arms hang as dead weights at the sides, or place them in various positions on the upper or lower chest to note chest expansion or diaphragmatic movements.

a. Inhale calmly through the nose, filling the abdominal cavity first and then the chest cavity. Exhale quietly.
b. Repeat this exercise by inhaling and exhaling through the mouth.
c. Inhale fully. Hold the breath while counting up to five mentally. Gradually increase the count.
d. Inhale rapidly through the nostrils. Exhale through the mouth.
e. Smell an imaginary or a real flower. Inhale as above.
f. Blow bubbles, puff balls, feathers, or blow up a rubber balloon.
g. Pretend that you are a limp rag doll.

With this much done, you should feel as you do when you finish warm-up exercises for jogging or swimming. Now you are ready to begin to talk.

Trust your past experience when you contemplate your usual audience. This vast but seldom tapped memory bank of everything you have ever experienced or read about is a vital factor in your success as a talker. No two people have had identical life experiences. Talk about them as your own source of private education. For instance, if in your childhood your family moved around a lot, you know that there is much to say about uprooting and adjusting to a new environment. This is a plus for you. You have survived. From all that relocating, you probably know how to make friends fast and easily, how to get a home or apartment into shape quickly, how to absorb new cultural patterns with little inconvenience.

Prepare to talk using informed opinion. The contacts you make and keep are valuable assets. "Rap" often with people who are experts in different fields. They'll be happy to tell you what they know. In fact, they are often made happy knowing that someone is interested in what they do. Read more than you need on every conceivable subject: current, historical, political, sensational, topical. Read more, however, on the subject you want to become an expert in, whether it relates to your present job or not. If your work is vitally interesting to you, keep updated on your reading in that area. It gives you a sense of personal advancement, and it can hold your spirit in high gear until promotions and raises come your way.

Practice. When you have decided what content will be included in the report you are to give at the business meeting, you have before you the tall task of organizing it so that it will float gracefully, like a swan on a lake. Be sure that you have decided upon the object of your talk and the audience reaction you hope for. You can have only one main topic. It must somehow be expressed to your hearers as simply and clearly as possible. Your topic can have subdivisions, but these must be tied into the main line in such a way that they either radiate from it or fit snugly into it. They should be clearly received as subsidiary features.

Gather your notes together and place your main idea on three by five-inch index cards. A manuscript form is also acceptable. Some talkers like to write out everything they expect to say, because they have a terrible fear of forgetting. Others feel bound to follow every word they see on the page; using the manuscript method, they have space to breathe and a guaranteed flow of language. If you choose to write out your entire talk, be sure you understand that the art of writing is not exactly the same as the art of speaking. For example, when Winston Churchill spoke these words after the British troops left Dunkirk, they were designed expressly to be *said:*

> . . . we shall defend our island, whatever the cost may be, we shall fight on the beaches, we shall fight on the landing grounds, we shall fight in the fields and in the streets, we shall fight in the hills; we shall never surrender.

If Churchill planned to write these words for a journal, rather than to speak them, he might have written:

> At all costs, we shall defend our island. We will fight on land and sea. And we will never surrender.

Notice that the forceful talker repeats his central message for his hearers. That is where the impact lies. Here is another example of writing words for diaries or books versus writing words to be heard live. Felix Schelling once said:

> True education makes for inequality: the inequality of individuality, the inequality of success; the glorious inequality of genius, of talent; for inequality, not mediocrity, individual superiority, not standardization, is the measure of the progress of the world.

If he wrote the same thought to be put in a book, he might have written:

> True education makes for the following kinds of wholesome and desirable inequality: success, genius, talent. Inequality is what makes for superior contributions to world progress.

When talking, your notes are the link between your words and your listeners. Be sure to prepare more than you think you need. Organize the notes according to value. Have one note support another, so that the flow of ideas will not be interrupted. An outline of your overall plan should be sketched before you begin the "heavy" work, or it can

be compiled at the end of your research, if your style is better suited
to that. An outline should look "cropped," because it is not supposed
to give detail. Here is a sample outline form:

I) Big idea
  A) Supporting idea(s)
    1. Specific examples

When the outline and the message content are finished, start talking
to yourself. Read and study your words carefully and hear in your
mind whether they make sense. Then read out loud to hear whether
your words make sense to your ears. If they do, read your talk before
a mirror, so that you can study the talker (yourself). If all seems well,
begin the rounds of asking others to listen to you. Make them promise
to be harsh critics. If they really don't like what they hear, you may
have to do some revising. Don't worry about this; it is best to catch
a blunder while it is still young. Other ears may not be as sympathetic
as your friends' ears.

Polish your talk. After your first practices, put your notes away.
Look at them again several hours or several days later, depending on
the amount of time you have before your talk. Now you will once
again have to find a way to make a good talk better. Go back to breathing
exercises. Start from scratch. Check your lung power.

The first rule of talk is that you be heard. If your lungs go weak
on you, do some additional practicing. Prolong your breath as long
as you can while saying these sounds:

Ah—oo   Ay—oo   M—ah   M—ay

Try arguing with someone you have been anxious to tell off. Notice
how bright the volume and how sharp and clear the words when people
argue. Listen to a mother scold her young child:

WHAT/TIME/DID/I/TELL/YOU/TO/BE/HOME?

People have wonderful diction when they are angry. That is because
they take better care of their words in a fight; they can't afford not

to be heard or understood. It matters too much that the message sent
is the message received. Lung power can be a fine friend in moments
of crisis. It can also be helpful for plain everyday talk. Keep developing
your lungs with sentences like:

Ship ahoy! (spoken to someone three feet away from you)
Ship ahoy! (spoken to someone twenty feet away from you)
Ship ahoy! (shouted to someone a block away from you)

The second rule of talk is that you be understood. A great deal of
faulty enunciation comes from lazy movements of one of the speech
organs or aids. For example, some people scarcely move the lower
jaw, thus failing to open the mouth. To demonstrate the effect of such
action, say a sentence holding the jaw almost rigid. Then repeat the
sentence using exaggerated movement of the lower jaw, noting the difference.

To increase the flexibility of the muscles used in talk, the following
exercises may be used. The tongue may be exercised by stretching. It
can be stretched straight out of the mouth, down, up, and sideways.
Roll the tongue, trill it, and make quick movements like those of a
cat lapping milk. For lip exercises, try biting them, puckering, smiling
broadly, and trilling. Jaw exercises include yawning and drills using
the sound "ah" combined with various consonants.

Having learned to make the best use of talk organs, you should
practice reading paragraphs very slowly, or saying rhymes, verses, or
rhyming couplets. Pay little attention to the thought. Concentrate on
word formation, with special emphasis on final "d" and "t" sounds.

You can polish your talk by being sure that you've caught the mood
you are after. Moods are certain atmospheres that can be created only
by the speaker. They are magic air waves over which you can convey
the tone that carries your message in the way you want. Tone or mood
can be made sharp by practicing with selections that have a definite
mood value. Read aloud the words of a mood master, Edgar Allen
Poe. Here is a passage from his short story "The Fall of the House
of Usher":

During the whole of a dull, dark and soundless day in the autumn
of the year, when the clouds hung oppressively low in the heavens,

I had been passing alone, on horseback, through a singularly dreary tract of country, and at length found myself, as the shades of the evening grew on, within view of the melancholy House of Usher. I know not how it was—but, with the first glimpse of the building, a sense of insufferable gloom pervaded my spirit. I say insufferable; for the feeling was unrelieved by any of that half-pleasurable, because poetic, sentiment with which the mind usually receives even the sternest natural images of the desolate or terrible. I looked upon the scene before me—upon the mere house, and the simple landscape figures of the domain—upon the bleak walls—upon the vacant eye-like windows—upon a few rank sedges—and upon a few white trunks of decayed trees—with an utter depression of soul . . .

Another way to polish your words and their effect on others is to observe carefully all the nuances you can achieve from simple punctuation. For example, a sign on the door of a barbershop in a small Southern town gave one message from the outside and another from the inside. Both messages contained the same words. The sign from outside read:

> What do you think
> We'll give you a shave
> And buy you a drink.

From the inside, the sign read:

> What? Do you think
> We'll give you a shave
> And buy you a drink?

Punctuation exists for the eye alone. There is meaning in your tone when you translate the punctuation marks. Tone sets the mood. There is the story of the guest talker who agreed to say a few words at a luncheon for a women's group on the subject:

> Woman—Without Her, Man Is a Savage

He prepared a humorous discussion and worked long and hard on getting just the right mood. His timing was fine, his examples were well chosen, his details were polished and easy on the ear. When he arrived at the restaurant where his guests were awaiting him, he found that, under his name on the program, was the title of his talk, typed thus:

Woman Without Her Man Is a Savage

This is another example of how punctuation can change entirely the meaning and the mood that you are trying to communicate.

Polishing your talk requires that you study where to add gestures, if any. Gestures are the conveyers and shapers of words in the same way that a conductor's baton moves an orchestra. Observe people who "talk with their hands." They wave them about until there is scarcely any meaning left in their movements. Gestures should affirm what you are saying and reinforce meaning. As a significant type of body-language, gestures have both universal and private meanings. The smile is an international gesture of approval, as the handshake is an international gesture of affability.

Head gestures are many and varied. Crossing one's eyes can be taken as either a sign of desperation or a comic twist. Shades of meaning are communicated to others through a nod, a wink, furrowed or relaxed eyebrows, listening with mouth open or closed, and the intensity of eye-touch. Many communication specialists hold that if any message is relayed from one to another, it is done through the eyes. People say that they don't feel at ease with someone who has "shifty" eyes. You label as suspicious people who won't look at you when they, or you, are talking or who slit their eyes to give you the once-over. When you speak, do you look directly into the centermost part of your listener's eyes? Or, in your anxiety, do you concentrate on the ceiling while your words, like dead sparks, fly aimlessly around the room? If you have more than one listener, you can tell by their facial expressions whether you are reaching them. For example, a math teacher who does a complicated problem at the blackboard had better "check in" with his students on the amount of information being received and understood by them. The teacher can know this only when he looks directly at the faces of his class. Frowns, wrinkled noses, or raised eyebrows are all the signals he needs.

Hand gestures are whole conversations in themselves. They are little streams of messages that flow from you to your hearers. The codes they usually convey are emotional in tone and should be used especially in the more emotional parts of your talk. We are all familiar with the standard hand gestures, like the woman who "throws up her hands in despair," or the man who "washes his hands of the whole affair." But what about the more subtle hand movements, like a sweeping gesture to indicate that all is lost? Consider the use of the hand to interrupt others. These gestures may range from placing a hand on the speaker's arm to pointing to your watch as a reminder that he's over the time limit.

You can tell what makes a person "go" by observing the total body gestures. An unhappy person usually shuffles along, head and shoulders bent, feet dragging, posture shaped like a question mark. We expect to see a person in uniform, especially military, walk snappily, briskly, with an air of confidence and authority. Deep thinkers can usually be spotted walking with hands clasped behind their backs, heads slightly bowed as if to be communicating with the good earth. The overbearing, pompous type of person has only to stride into our presence with head and chin raised abnormally high, arms swinging too far and too wide, and we know him for what he is.

All things considered, it is better to polish the gestures you want to make when you talk, rather than to make random movements that have nothing to do with what you are saying. The trick to remember here is to make the gestures simple, large enough, and very definite. End them precisely. Don't let them trail away like a wisp of smoke. Some talkers pound the podium or the desk. If you intend to say something startling, like "Give me liberty or give me death," a good strong gesture of defiance would do nicely. So would a firm, strong whisper of absolute certainty and conviction.

For practice in the polishing of gestures, here are some simple sentences for you to experiment with. Vocalize with body actions for the greatest effect.

Okay, let 'em go!
You just don't know what we've been through!
Come here!

How much?
It's nonsense!
You may pick it up, but handle it with care.
I loved the excitement, but I'm very tired.
Isn't that a beautiful sight?
We'll fight this injustice to the bitter end.
Will you please give me more time to do the exercise?
I reject that plan as impractical and inappropriate.
On the lower level of the veranda, the roof was gabled.
The ground was covered here and there with patches of ice.
I ask you for the last time to consider my offer.
There are just two questions to be answered: first, do we need a change? and second, is this change the right one?

Present your talk. When you are actually in the process of talking, keep a constant check on how you are doing. You can easily find out by surveying the face or faces of your listeners. Remember, the eyes say it all. If they are shut tight, you should devise a plan called "Wake up."

This calls for a little ingenuity. You may have to come up with a startling introduction that serves as a link between you and your listeners and among the listeners themselves. For instance, if you are talking in "pep rally" fashion to a few letter carriers about stepping up production, you could open with "Down with mailmen!" Then add softly, "said an old crank who neither sends nor receives letters." Your introduction, which works out to be about 10 percent of any talk, should grab your audience with such lightning speed that they have no choice but to want to hear more.

What's your big idea? You should have one bright central idea each time you speak professionally. (Remind yourself that a professional is anyone who knows what he or she is talking about.) Having more than one idea confuses people.

Why are you talking about your subject? Have you been invited to speak by popular demand? Did your boss or teacher or president of the local fire fighters union insist that you say a few words to the group gathered together tonight? If so, trust their judgment in asking you, and say to yourself: "If not you, who? If not now, when?" On the other hand, if you have invited yourself, say, in an interview situation, you should be all the more eager to sell yourself through techniques you have practiced faithfully.

When you are about to conclude, remember to give some sign to the audience that you are ready to wind things up. It could be a summary statement, a quotation, an illustration of your "big idea," a personal anecdote. Psychologically, your hearers need to know when you are preparing for a grand finale.

When you talk, there are other considerations that have to do with your listeners. You must judge how emotional they will be in relation to you and your topic. If you speak of religion or politics contrary to the persuasion of the majority of your audience, you will have a rough time of it. They will not, at first, be open-minded to your words. If your group is mixed, however, everyone can enjoy a good shaking up. Be sure to know how to temper your words so as not to alienate your hearers. Remember, everyone can be reached. You may need to be less formal than you prepared to be, after you have seen the composition of your group. Physically, you may want to move nearer to them. In fact, you might like to rearrange the order of the room and make a circle of the rows of chairs.

Before you do this, check to see if the room itself imposes any limitations on you. If it is a large, barnlike space, close proximity is a must. If the room is small, you can arrange any spatial grouping quite easily. Your tone is important, too. Volume needs to be turned up for high ceilings and wide walls. It can be turned down or "naturalized" for ski lodges and fireplace audiences.

When presenting your polished piece, ask yourself if you will have more than one opportunity to talk to this particular group. If you are to see them again, be sure to leave them wanting more. You have to put twice as much effort into being successful if you will be standing before these listeners again tomorrow and on Thursday.

Sounds Like

Because sounds make up words, we can assume that if we say parts of a word well, it will follow that we can say the whole word well.

With this in mind, it shouldn't be too difficult to do some helpful exercises in behalf of sounds. Even non-sense is sound, and from sound comes sense—eventually. Set aside some time to do these vocal gymnastics at your leisure and for your pleasure. They will lead you to professional talk—in time.

It is noticeable that unusual sounds without meaning and various refrains have a particular fascination for all. Practice them for the fun of it, and in so doing the desired flexibility and adroitness for the talk organs will result.

Repeat each column as rapidly as possible. Stop for breath only when you need it.

ped-dl-ty—ded-dl-ty	ad-dl-ty—dad-dl-ty
bid-dl-ty—did-dl-ty	ar-ker-ty—kar-ker-ty
min-nim-in—nim-min-im	ag-ger-dy—gag-er-dy
fad-dl-ty—dad-dl-ty	et-ter-ty—tet-er-ty
kak-kl-ty—gag-gl-ty	ad-jer-dy—jad-jar-dy
wo-ker-ty—yo-ker-ty	ush-er-shy—shus-er-shy
rush-er-ty—slush-er-ty	ur-rer-ry—rur-rer-ry
grim-per-ty—klim-per-ty	with-ith-thy—tith-ith-thy
nun-der-y—dun-der-y	is-si-kis—sik-is-is
plum-per-ty—glum-per-ty	ish-shi-gish—shi-gi-shis
flat-er-ty—tat-er-ty	pip-per-ty—tip-per-ty
pip-er-ty—tip-per-ty	

Say each of the following lines distinctly and rapidly without stopping:

pipe-pip-poppy-puppy-punch-piper-pull-pumper
bid-barb-baby-bud-bubble-blabber-blubber
mammy-move-must-murmur-much-mimic
four-five-fifty-fireflies-fluffy-flitting
vine-vain-vivid-voice-virtue-very-varied
tip-top-tough-tittle-tattle-titter-twitter
did-dub-daddy-dupe-dodder-dawdling-donkey
let-light-illumine-lily-lolling-little-lamb

now-new-never-ninny-nearly-nonny-nanny
rose-row-hurry-rude-rearing-roaring-rising
king-kind-kooky-kinky-cockle-cold-cocoa
gag-gig-gun-giggle-gargle-guggle-gagger
see-sun-set-suspend-assassin-sassy-sassafras
zeal-zion-zone-zigzag-zulu-zero
will-well-won-weaver-water-washer
sham-shoe-shirt-shrinking-shutter-shimmer
church-chum-chicken-cheat-cheerful-chatter

Take some additional moments to round out your practice polishing
"ing" sounds. The following exercise is a sequence from a poem by
Robert Southey. It is especially designed to help those of us who cheat
on "ing" words. We all know someone who says

I wuz walkin on the beach, walkin and talkin and singin with some
friends, when I saw this guy whistlin and walkin toward us . . .

The words that follow will cure the incurable. They are from "The
Cataract of Lodore."

Dividing and sliding and gliding,
And falling and brawling and sprawling,
And driving and riving and striving,
And sprinkling and twinkling and wrinkling,
And sounding and bounding and rounding,
And bubbling and troubling and doubling,
And grumbling and rumbling and tumbling,
And clattering and battering and shattering,
Retreating and beating and meeting and sheeting,
Delaying and straying and playing and spraying,
Advancing and prancing and glancing and dancing,
Recoiling and turmoiling and toiling and boiling,
And gleaming and steaming and streaming and beaming,
And rushing and flushing and brushing and gushing,
And flapping and rapping and clapping and slapping,

And curling and whirling and purling and twirling,
And thumping and plumping and bumping and jumping,
And dashing and flashing and splashing and clashing,
And so never ending, but always descending,
Sounds and motion forever are blending,
All at once and all o'er, with a mighty uproar,
And this way the water comes down at Lodore.

The next exercise is one in concentration and diction, the purpose being the ultimate clarity of each word. There is actually some sense in this nonsense paragraph. Read it carefully for both sound and sense.

Esau Wood sawed wood. Esau Wood would saw wood. All the wood Esau Wood saw Esau Wood would saw. In other words, all the wood Esau saw to saw Esau sought to saw. Oh, the wood Wood would saw! And oh! the wood-saw with which Wood would saw wood. But one day Wood's wood-saw would saw no wood, and thus the wood Wood sawed was not the wood Wood would saw if Wood's wood-saw would saw wood. Now, Wood would saw wood with a wood-saw that would saw wood; so Esau sought a saw that would saw wood. One day Esau saw a saw saw wood as no other wood-saw Wood saw would saw wood. In fact, of all the wood-saws Wood ever saw saw wood Wood never saw a wood-saw that would saw wood as the wood-saw Wood saw saw wood, and I never saw a wood-saw that would saw as the wood-saw Wood saw would saw until I saw Esau saw wood with the wood-saw Wood saw saw wood. Now Wood saws wood with the wood-saw Wood saw saw wood.

In the following practice work, the sounds make sense. As you tackle them, be sure not to skimp on any syllable of any word. The correct pronunciation of each word is a bonus for you as a successful talker.

1. Bill had a billboard. Bill also had a board bill. The board bill bored Bill so that Bill sold the billboard to pay the board bill. Now the board bill no longer bores Bill.
2. What whim led Will Whitney to whittle, whistle and whisper near the wharf where a floundering whale might wheel and whirl?

3. Six long slim slick slender saplings.
4. The shiny silk sashes shimmered when the sun shone on the shop.
5. Esau saw the buck and the buck saw Esau.
6. Washington's washwoman washed Washington's wash while Washington washed Wilson.
7. Susan sells seashells on the seashore.
8. Amidst the mists and coldest fronts,
   With stoutest wrists and loudest boasts,
   He thrusts his fists against the posts,
   And still insists he sees the ghosts.
9. Algy met a bear. The bear was bulgy, and the bulge was Algy.
10. A tree toad loved a she-toad
    That lived up in a tree.
    She was a three-toed she-toad.
    But a two-toed tree-toad tried to win
    The she-toad's friendly nod.
    For the two-toed tree toad loved the ground
    That the three-toed she-toad trod.
11. Some shun sunshine. Do you shun sunshine?
12. Twenty timid toads trying to trot to Trenton.
13. The sun shines on the shop signs.
14. The seething sea ceaseth and it sufficeth me.
15. If to hoot and to toot a Hottentot tot
    Were taught by a Hottentot tutor,
    Should the tutor get hot if the Hottentot tot
    Should hoot and toot at the tutor?
16. Betty bought a bit of butter,
    "But," said she, "this butter's bitter.
    If I put it in my batter, it will make my batter bitter."
    So Betty bought a bit of better butter,
    Put it in her batter and made her batter better.

A final practice in learning to discriminate between sounds will serve to sharpen your word flow until it becomes a finely tuned instrument. Say each of the following sentences as carefully and distinctly as possible.

1. Paul prepared to clip the paper tape.
2. The drab ebony board was buried above the neighbor's lab.
3. Lemons make Tom remember many moments of gloom.
4. One never knows how many cannons are necessary.
5. I think that running ink is distinctive.
6. Peter takes teeter-tottering too seriously.
7. An unthoughtful but enthusiastic thinker in math gave baby Dora a bath.
8. Fifty-five and one-half fifes filled Phil's safe.
9. "Very lovely voice," answered Eve from above.
10. Chimpanzees lurched in bunches by the church but did not chortle much.
11. George jumped over Roger to juggle the gauge.
12. Walter, overweight but unworried, ate Wilma's sandwich willfully.
13. The left-handed hermit followed the fox hunter uphill.
14. The terrible rapids passed the bar very readily.

Imagination: Your Speech Survival Kit

Good talk comes from fast thinking. Fast thinking happens when the imagination is allowed to work on a full-time basis. Unlike the rest of the animate world, human beings share a phenomenal gift in common. Imagination is both a gift and a talent. Like language, it needs to be cultivated. Our imaginations run free and unrestricted when we're very young. Unhappily, as we grow older, we tend to hold back on the bubbling, spontaneous flow of ideas and images that were our constant companions in childhood. Our imaginations are uniquely brilliant and one of a kind like diamonds. All the facets sparkle with original colors and shapes. The sparkle becomes even more lustrous with the passage of time.

When talking your way to the top, your hope should lie in the free, unlimited use of your imaginative powers. Start now to "let go" in the way of unusual, even off-beat, ideas. Those who move ahead fastest in life continually trust themselves to come up with different, even zany or preposterous, ideas. The people with ideas move up. How can you start a rusty imagination on the road to recovery? Here are some ways.

Experiment with language that is unfamiliar or is accented with an unusual dialect. Take an old-fashioned fairy tale and infuse it with a coded language all its own. "The Big Lion and the Little Mouse" could be revised to read "The Lig Bion and the Mittle Louse." It would continue thus:

> Once upon a time a lig bion was fying last asleep in the weep doods when a mittle louse came bunning ry. Alas for the mee wouse. She ran right over the bighty meast's nose!

> Translation: Once upon a time a big lion was lying fast alseep in the deep woods when a little mouse came running by. Alas for the wee mouse. She ran right over the mighty beast's nose!

Other familiar tales such as "Rindercella and the Cince" and "Little Ride Hooding Red" can provide an imaginative adventure if pursued for the pure delight of it. Foreign accents, too, expand the imagination. The use of accents requires a keen ear and sharp powers of observation. Here is a small portion of "Goldilocks and the Three Bears" in a new light.

> Uns appona taim uas tre berrese; mamma berre, papa berre, e baibi berre. Dey live inna contri nire foresta. Naise aus. Nu mugheggia. Una die papa, mama e baibi go beecha for die, e forghetta locche di dorre.

> Translation: Once upon a time was three bears; mama bear, papa bear, and baby bear. They live in the country near a forest. Nice house. No mortgage. One day papa, mama and baby go to the beach for the day, and forget to lock the door.

In the same mode, take some familiar poems and reset them in a new pattern of speech. How would Wordsworth's famous poem sound if we spoke it in another key? As in a hall of mirrors, the literal meaning would be distorted into many strange shapes and sizes. This is a good

workout for your voice, and it challenges the imagination to do things
it would otherwise never think of. Let us "play" with Wordsworth
and see what new shapes, colors, and meanings appear.

> Thee whirled a stew much widows. Latent soon
> Get in and spend din, Willie way star pars.
> Little we sea innate chew rat is sours.
> Weave give an hour arts a weight, assorted boon.
> This seethe at bears Sir Booze hum to thumb moon,
> The win zat Will B. Howell in gat awl lowers
> Endor up gat heard an owl Ike's leaping flowers,
> For this, forever wreathing weir rout of tune;
> It moves us knock. Greek hod! I'd rather be
> A pig unsuckled in a cree doubt warn
> So my tie stand in honest pleasantly
> Have glim, says Atwood, make mealless furl on,
> Have sigh to approaches rye sing from the sea
> Or Harold try to unblow his wreath adorn.

Now try reading the poem so as to convey to an audience the meaning
Wordsworth sought to express:

> The world is too much with us; late and soon,
> Getting and spending, we lay waste our powers:
> Little we see in nature that is ours;
> We have given our hearts away, a sordid boon!
> This sea that bares her bosom to the moon;
> The winds that will be howling at all hours,
> And are up-gather'd now like sleeping flowers;
> For this, for everything, we are out of tune;
> It moves us not.—Great God! I'd rather be
> A Pagan suckled in a creed outworn;
> So might I, standing on this pleasant lea,
> Have glimpses that would make me less forlorn;
> Have sight of Proteus rising from the sea;
> Or hear old Triton blow his wreathèd horn.

Your imagination can also be put to good practice by taking common objects, such as a simple wire coat hanger, and naming as many uses for it as you can. Here is a very partial listing:

radio, TV, lightning rod antenna
mobile, wire sculpture, wall decoration
pipe cleaner, vacuum hose cleaner, drain cleaner
eggbeater, ice pick
bird cage
rafter-reacher, fishing rod
fastener for a bundle of wood
fishhook
series of loops in a fence
frame or support for Christmas wreath, garden plant, wall decoration
doorstop, window stop
holder for cards, magazines, loose papers, books, paintbrushes
paint stirrer
lock-pick
back-scratcher
trap for animals

To stretch your imagination to its widest reaches, do mental workouts while you are riding in a bus or waiting for the light to change. Begin with a simple hypothetical phrase like "What if . . . ?" Finish the phrase with as many sensible and sensational possibilities as you are tempted with. Don't think. Just let your ideas tumble and roll fresh from their source. What if we had a third arm? What if we walked on our hands continually? What if every fourth person in the world were two inches tall? What if every third apartment building were made of cotton candy? What if the force of gravity propelled objects upward, rather than downward? What if grass and shrubs were plaid or purple? What if there were no colors in the world?

When you tire of the "What if . . . ?" puzzle, start imagining new possibilities for yourself as a talker. Always be on the lookout for ways to extend the range and scope of your ideas. Think about a problem that you've been mulling over for some time. Rephrase the problem in as many ways as you can without losing the essential meaning. Sometimes a different approach to a question can produce the enlightenment you have looked for.

Your imagination lights up by itself when you have the chance to be alone with it. There is never a split second of time when your mind is blank, dull, empty, thinking of nothing. Even consciously thinking of nothing is thinking of something. Challenge your best ideas as you walk along the beach or as you ride for a few moments in an elevator. Phenomenal, isn't it, that few of us ever look with wonder upon commonplace occurrences? Take the simple *act* of elevator-riding. Think how unusual it is to be suspended by a cable or two in a metal box that goes up and down, carrying strangers on private missions to separate destinies. Begin to see the common happenings of everyday life as something wonderful and unfamiliar. The writer Henry David Thoreau took years out of his life to be by himself and live near a pond in the woods. He did this, not because he was a shy person who felt unconfident, but because he needed to "see" the things he had taken for granted in a new and luminous light. His perspective was restored after months of observing even the smallest leaf or the minutest woodland creature. He knew that we get so carried away with unimportant daily tasks that we need to have our eyes "dry cleaned" from time to time.

Ideas flow when we give them a life of their own. No one can ever take from you what is yours for the wishing. Observe details of people, events, concepts. Add your own measure of embellishment to what already exists in the world. Trust the red balloon of your imagination to serve you well. You won't be disappointed.

How To Say Better Than Average Words Without Being a Show-off

When you're good, you don't have to say it. Your hearers know it. How can you be a cut above the rest and not come off as a conceited, self-centered know-all? Well, for starters, as long as you are convinced of your own strength and capabilities, you are ahead by a long shot. Following fast on the heels of self-belief is the need for quick assessment of your listeners. Ask yourself what most of them have in common. Are they united by age, sex, ability, temperament, occupation, profession? When you know the common bond, you can talk accordingly. What is your relationship to them? If you are a friend, the better for you. A nice touch is to shake the hand of your listeners, fasten your eyes upon theirs at the same time, and convey the message that each of them matters personally to you—more, that each of them makes a difference in your life. This is true. You are never the same person you were before you met John or Peggy this afternoon.

Ask yourself how much your listeners already know of the subject about to be discussed. Be able to lock into their level immediately. You can approximate the starting point by having obtained background information about your audience before you meet with them. You can also obtain this information by talking informally with them before the discussion. You must also find out how much more they want to know. In the give-and-take exchange of information, you have an allotted amount of time to get things done. Do only what is feasible to do. The world is not going to stop turning on its axis if you don't accomplish all your plans for the hour or the day. Sometimes talk, if it's good, takes unplanned directions, with more profit coming from the new direction than from the old plan.

A show-off is often asking for a showdown. The simple secret of pleasing others is to be honest, sincere, direct, open. It works every time. If you are anxious or nervous, say so. Weaknesses are human and extremely endearing to other human beings. Having admitted to them is a bonus of admiration for you.

Terror Strikes

You know the feeling: a hard knot in the pit of the stomach, a lump in the throat that can't be swallowed away. Instant death would be a happier prospect than facing your fellow sales managers with the quarterly report. It's not that you don't have the facts and figures at the ready. You know the material, all right. Too bad you can't stay at home and speak your words into a tape recorder. You could mail in the tape, and your four area managers could listen to your message without seeing you tremble and shake.

The anxiety that precedes talking to a live person before you is as common as insomnia is to bank robbers. There are, however, several ways to live in harmony with your nervous system. If you ignore it, it won't go away. Learn to deal with it as a friendly foe. Here are some ideas.

1. The more you talk, the easier it becomes to talk well. Don't pass up any opportunity to communicate effectively. Although it isn't the easiest of all possible tasks, talking well can be more rewarding in the long run than doing many other things well.

2. If you ever have a chance, allow yourself to be videotaped in the act of talking. You can see exactly how you look and act. If you slouch, mumble, talk to only one part of your audience, or fix your eyes firmly on the ceiling, it will be recorded by the unerring lens. This is a fine way to practice anxiety control. You may not come off as poorly as you think you do.

3. You must believe that there is no such thing as a boring person. If you have to change the way you feel about yourself and your achievements, then do it. You *always* have something worthwhile to communicate to someone else. You become panicky when you feel that you aren't interesting, or that you don't know much, or that you have absolutely nothing to say. This attitude paints a pretty bleak picture, and a false one at that.

4. Relax into your talk. If you find relaxing difficult, remember that it is always possible to breathe yourself calm. Here are some additional exercises for you to do when terror strikes.

Inhale comfortably until you "pack the lungs" with air. Keep your mouth closed and breathe from your rib-cage down, so that when you exhale it feels like a balloon deflating. Feel free to shout, grunt, and flail your arms about wildly as you attempt to rid yourself of tension. Deep breathing helps you to eliminate carbon dioxide from your body. You need to detoxify yourself in order to be composed.

5. Remind yourself continually that you are polishing a desperately needed skill. You are trying to elevate the gift of talk to an art form. You are doing all this because you know that people get ahead by communicating well, and they stay behind by communicating obscurely. You also know that success is the product of hard work and the determination to achieve. You need people to communicate with. Some of

those people can see you to the top of the mountain of your goals. Why not do well what nature has begun in you? It is a good thing to recall that anything worthwhile is usually hard to come by. Whenever you talk with anyone, be it matron, maitre d', or magistrate, assure yourself that it would be easier to be reporting the local baseball game from the stadium than it is to stand before a judge arguing yourself out of a parking ticket. The *reason* that talking into a microphone is simpler than talking to a live person lies in the realm of eye-contact. You don't need it for broadcasting from a booth. You *do* need it to argue your cause with anyone face to face. The difference is essential to your future.

6. You know that most physical fear responses have logical explanations. Your heart may sound like drums in the night because you forgot to prepare your words. Your breathing may be irregular because you didn't find out about the composition of your audience: age, education, ability. You might feel your face redden into a deep blush because you have been studying the overhead fixtures rather than fixing your eyes on your guests.

7. Remember that all normal persons experience fear when they are faced with doing any worthwhile project. Think of the great fears that loom within the hearts of soldiers before the heat of battle. How about the climbers who scaled Mount Everest? Or the first astronauts to the moon? Fear can be useful to you if you keep your goal in sight. Having a normal anxiety level when you talk is good because it keeps the vital adrenalin flowing.

8. A final rule on talk-fright. The more you practice, the easier the job of talking becomes. Fear is normal and can be considered a friend. If your fears are overwhelming, perhaps the fault is yours for not doing your homework.

In sum, fear can be tempered with the joy of knowing a job well done. It can polish your delivery, enhance your image, achieve your goal. The polish you acquire from taking the time to do it right—that is, to talk yourself from a mediocre state to a better one, or to talk to others as if your future and theirs were of real concern to you—will be well worth the effort.

CHAPTER IV

Word-Watching

"I don't know what you mean by 'glory'," Alice said. Humpty Dumpty smiled contemptuously. "Of course you don't—till I tell you. I meant 'there's a nice knock-down argument for you!' "

"But 'glory' doesn't mean 'a nice knock-down argument,' " Alice objected.

"When I use a word," Humpty Dumpty said, in a rather scornful tone, "it means just what I choose it to mean—neither more nor less."

"The question is," said Alice, "whether you *can* make words mean so many different things."

"The question is," said Humpty Dumpty, "which is to be master— that's all."

—Lewis Carroll

Word-watching is akin to people-watching, and it is an exciting game to play. Word-watching can also be beneficial in advancing your profession or career. The word is all-important before and after the deed. When you watch words you are aware of more than what the word means. You are additionally aware of what the person saying the word means. In fact, word-watching can be the key to your survival in a competitive society.

In order to be an accomplished word-watcher, you must read a lot, talk a lot, and listen a lot. You will know that a word which held a certain meaning five or ten years ago may hold a different meaning today. Our language is in a constant state of repair and revision. Although some stability in language, especially at the roots, is needed if we are to continue to survive by our wits, we should be aware of the changing nature of the words around us.

Our Changing Language

Here is a bit from the conversation of an eighteen-year-old who is hopeful of communicating a vital message to his friend.

Joe: Hey, man, wot a week. Oh, wow!
Moe: Outasight, huh?
Joe: Like wow, man. I had a hassle with the parkway cops, and a worse hassle when I got home. My boss gave me a hassle at work, and I had to hassle the business office about receipts and stuff like that. Man, this week was the pits.
Moe: Far out.

Such attempts at communicating are quite common in our everyday abuse of words. If Joe really wanted to get through to the mind of his friend, he would have spelled out in detail what, *exactly,* he meant by the word "hassle." All his friend could surmise was that Joe didn't have a good week. What happened on the highway, what unpleasantness took place at home, and what kind of difficulties Joe encountered at work and at the business office are vague and uncertain. In other words, the word "hassle," by trying to mean so many things, has come to mean nothing at all.

Moe should know that, if he wants to be precise when he talks, he had better define his terms. "Out of sight" literally means "beyond the range of vision." If Joe had a week that was beyond his range of vision, it was a week that he literally couldn't see. If so, how does it tie in with all his unlucky episodes? Those he surely could see and feel. To have lived through a week that was "the pits" is a challenge indeed, since the phrase "in the pits" originated when some addicts, having used up all available veins for the injection of their drugs, resorted to the armpits in a desperate attempt to find new veins.

Word-watching implies that we take long hard looks at meanings. If we question the value of certain words, we can avoid the pitfall of overusing a catch-all word because we don't have the desire or the ambition to find a better one. If we want people to "take us at our word," it had better be the right word with a meaning all its own.

The better job, the bigger raise, the fatter bonus, and the greater challenges will certainly accrue to the person who can say, "It is a great pleasure to be of service to your company. I am available at your convenience." A bright future is not in order for the one who says, "Like man, it's neat to work here. So call me when you've got some work."

Here are some words and phrases to watch as you begin your "Project Alert."

Meaningful. Everything in this world is meaningful. To put it another way, there is nothing that is meaningless to everyone. Is a "meaningful" experience one that led you to a richer life, one that helped you to grow inwardly, or one that you wish had never happened?

Relevant. This word is popular as a substitute for "meaningful." It is a vague word meant to represent a host of meanings. "Relevant" should mean "timely" or relating to the present, but it has come to mean "interesting, significant, pleasurable."

They say. Who are "they"? If "they" are a group of doctors, which group, how many physicians, who? If "they" are a group of mothers, what is the age range, how many children do they have, and so on.

Engaged. This word can mean pledged to marry or being busy. "I'm sorry, but she's engaged right now," needs to be clarified for the hearer.

Red tape. Is this a special kind of adhesive tape, as distinguished from other colors? Is there blue tape, green tape? Is "red tape" synonymous with the difficulty of getting answers in a bureaucratic system?

How do you do? How do you do what? When you are introduced to someone, the standard reply is, "How do you do?" Sometimes, in frustration, people have been heard to mutter "I exist," or "I continue."

Blah, blah, blah. People use this expression when they don't have the right words to finish the sentence. It is a substitute for the bygone "et cetera."

Late. This word is used in two entirely different ways. Late can mean deceased or after the time you were supposed to be at a certain place.

Whatsisface. This word has replaced "whatsisname" when you can't remember a person's name. It says that you couldn't care less about identifying the person.

Would you believe? This is a common catch-all phrase that signifies nothing. "I don't believe it!" is the expected response. A phrase of this sort says much more than three words. It is a sign of the times. "Would you believe?" really suggests that every event in our lives is unbelievable, incredible, beyond the range of ordinary experience. Whereas in years gone by truly uncommon events were reserved for books like Ripley's *Believe It Or Not* or the *Guinness Book of Records,* the unbelievable has become a common occurrence in household patter. For example, if a housewife wins three boxes of detergent on a television game show, she jumps up and down and screams jubilantly, "I don't believe it!" It follows, then, that if the commonplace is to be sensationalized in this generation, we will have no words left to describe a truly catastrophic event. In the event of a nuclear conflict or radiation fallout, we would have a pitiful handful of words available to accurately describe the human dilemma. Perhaps some spokesperson for our hypothetical plight would be videotaped sitting all alone on a curbstone, muttering: "Man. What a hassle. Like this is the pits. Oh, wow. I don't believe it."

You better believe it. This is a variant of the "Would you believe?" theme. It means that you are being told something altogether startling and earth-shaking. Should you have doubts, you show little sign of enjoying such a "meaningful" conversation.

Super. This word has come to mean new highs and impossible fulfillment of impossible expectations. "Super," in its latest connotation, means an absolute rejection of the word "average," which, in turn, has come to mean "mediocre." We no longer have "stars" performing on the Broadway stage and the filmscreen. If you are not a "superstar," you are a mediocre performer, or worse, a flunkie. In sports we have "superplayers," meaning that they are uncommonly well qualified athletes. Why this disdain for the word "average"? "Average" should mean "fulfills the necessary requirements of a job or challenge; gives satisfactory performance." No one wants to be "average" anymore because it means "low man on the totem pole." "Average" has become synonymous with "slow" or "retarded." People are insulted if they have "average" tastes and "average" abilities. If you can't be a supermom, why bother with motherhood at all? Perhaps the concept of "Superman" has to do with exceeding your own limitations. Or is it a rejection of the normal, everyday routine whereby we work a little to get ahead on the "average" scale? The "average" person should become respectable again. He or she is the hard worker, the believer in self, and the mover, shaker, and doer of things tomorrow. If you can do satisfactory work honestly, you will be needed and wanted to shape the conditions of the next generation.

Get your act together. This phrase is fast losing face, but it means, before it dies out finally, to "shape up or ship out." All new clichés have their origin in some worn-out one. New phrases always come on as overthrow and wind up as the coalition. "Getting your act together" simply means that if you are not qualified you won't get the job.

This has to be . . . This *has* to be the most meaningless phrase ever coined. "Has to be" means that by decision of the speaker, the conclusion of the phrase is an infallible statement replete with conclusive evidence. For example, "This *has* to be the worst party I've ever attended." Or "This *has* to be the longest hour of my life." To the latter lament, only one response is possible. All hours are sixty minutes, and this hour, bad as it may seem, is no longer or shorter than any other hour of time known to mankind.

Right on! Right on what? This cliché has caught on with lightning speed. Like every other movement in the language wave, it will have spent its energies before its arrival is generally recognized. It means "I agree with you," which is rapidly being replaced by "I couldn't agree more." If you are really "hep," "Right on!" should be accompanied by the appropriate gesture of the upturned thumb.

Rip-off. This is a popular idiom used for just about everything we feel we've been cheated of. Education has become a rip-off, public transportation is a rip-off, institutions and professions are flourishing as rip-off agencies. We can even be ripped off in our affections, as when one person sues another in divorce court. The phrase is a response to the spiraling inflationary condition. It really means that we can't keep up with rising costs.

Whatever. This neat little word has come to mean nothing because its value is so broad-based. ". . . or whatever" is a common phrase used to conclude our sentences when we can't think of appropriate words to put them to rest. Sometimes you hear a double "whatever," which requires a greater emphasis of voice, as in: "We'll go to Hawaii this summer, or whatever, whatever." People wear "whatever" to cocktail parties. They pay "whatever" to baby-sitters for a night out, or "whatever." Be careful of lapsing into the "whatever" syndrome. It can drive people crazy, and it tells them precious little about yourself except that you don't communicate very clearly.

Consciousness raising. This phrase is a sign of the times because it is coupled with the new "awareness" trends. In order to be a productive member of contemporary society, I must be "aware" of how I feel, how I look, and how I'm coming across to others at all times. "Consciousness raising" implies that my life until now has been spent in a state of semiconsciousness or total unconsciousness. We must attend consciousness-raising groups to help our plants grow greener and taller, to help our clothes look brighter and cleaner, to help our families love us more because we are more "aware" of them. Under the heading of "consciousness" or "awareness" the word "inner" is also associated. There is "inner tennis," which implies that tennis can be played inside your head, and "inner cooking," which allows you to thoroughly internalize the act of steaming vegetables and shucking corn.

Yecch! This has become the household word to replace "I don't like that," or "No, thank you." When asked if the movie was enjoyable or if the barbeque was done just right, "Yecch!" is the response of the inarticulate who find it difficult to say why they reject or refuse something.

Something else. "He's really something else," or "That's really something else," means literally that the person or idea we are referring to is really *not* the person or idea we are referring to, but another person or idea. If you are "something else," are you also "someone else"? Are objects and people as interchangeable as pears and onions?

Turn on or *turn off.* This, as we know, doesn't apply to the television set. It implies that human beings are robots, and as such can be made to "light up" on cue or walk away from a situation that leaves us cold.

Let it all hang out. This means that we are encouraged to spend our emotions and feelings as they present themselves to us. For example, if the desire to stand on top of the World Trade Center and shout our lungs out is overwhelming, we are invited to do just that. If a particular person's mannerisms are irritating to us, we are urged to tell that person how we feel. Letting ourselves "hang out" is akin to the time-worn "Do your own thing." Doing things of your own is really nothing new. People have been doing things by and for themselves since the dawn of civilization.

Out of the closet. This means that you have decided to be honest about the circumstances of your life. Why being "in a closet" makes a sneak of you is not quite clear, unless the metaphor of a closet being a dark, closed space is supposed to mean all you want it to mean.

Fantastic. The word has become a synonym for "incredible," which is a synonym for "super," which are synonyms for "out of sight" and "far out."

I know where you are coming from. This expression, along with "I can relate to it," simply means "I understand you." Where you come from—Southeast Asia or the Pacific Northwest—has nothing to do with it. If you can "relate" to something, you are able to make sense in a complicated word-jungle.

Our Changing Self

To grow is to change, and to have changed often is to have grown much.

—John Henry Newman

Because you have survived from yesterday until today, you are not the same person you were a mere twenty-four hours ago. Consider the advancements you have made in your life within the past year, the past month, the past week, the past hour.

Your personal progress and new directions are reflected in the language you choose in order to express your thoughts and feelings in the clearest possible way. In recent years, certain trends in word usage have crept into most of our vocabularies. One of the major thrusts has been the employment of euphemisms. Euphemisms are words or expressions that substitute a pleasant-sounding image for an unpleasant happening in life. The form that a language takes determines how the people who speak it perceive reality. For example, we all know that someday we will die. It is not a happy thought for most people, but it is an inescapable truth of life. The vocabulary we use to announce and describe the phenomenon of death has changed over the years from the simple statement "He died," to "He has expired, passed away."

"Count to a Thousand, Stay Away From the Phone, and Have a Nice Day."

Undertakers are being replaced by funeral directors or morticians. These, in turn, are being converted to grief therapists, as a result of the heavy emphasis on coming to terms with personal feelings.

Language that evaluates or judges certain deviant behavior patterns has become positive, even praiseful, in its expression of this type of behavior. For example, a juvenile delinquent is defined as a young person who has been delinquent, that is, who has *not* done something. Here are some report-card descriptions of unacceptable behavior patterns exhibited by an unruly child in the classroom.

Precise Description	*Euphemism*
Lazy	Needs appropriate supervision to enable him to complete assignment.
Disliked by everyone	Needs help in forming permanent relationships.
Dishonest	Could use value-systems instructional approach to acquaint him with acceptable modes of behavior.
Slow learner	Needs abundant remedial reinforcement with positive approach.

As we grow older, we tend to slip into patterns of obscurity in language. We think we should "impress," and we forget the most important rules of talk: be simple, clear, direct; be heard, be understood. Say what you mean. Mean exactly what you say.

As your changing self continues to grow, stop and reflect on whether or not your prejudices have been altered or discarded for the most part. We see what we have been programmed to see. We continue to label people and place them in certain preconceived categories. We call studious people "four-eyes" because we have seen a few bright people who also happen to wear glasses. We think of overweight people as sluggish and not vivacious, athletic, or energetic. What about the person who wears an eyepatch or tattoo? We say all too readily that he contributes to the underworld of crime or petty misdeeds. Take another look at the bleached blonde wearing a miniskirt. We wonder what she does on weekends. We label a man with severely constricted eyesight a blind man. We never think that he might also be an excellent typist, a superb husband and father, a terrific teacher and lecturer. We say that people with undesirable or dishonorable discharges from the Armed Forces must be unacceptable in life outside the military. We label as weird someone who does not think, feel, move, speak, or believe as we do.

What about the language of various ethnic groups? Consider the young girl from Havana, Cuba, who referred to her toes as "fingers of the foot." Ponder the dialogue between an old man in Dublin, Ireland, and a young woman seeking directions.

She: Do you know the way to the Embankment?
He: I do, yes. (He turns and walks on. End of conversation.)
She: (Runs after him to renew the conversation.) Can you tell me how to get there?
He: If I could I would. But you can't get there from here.

There is confusion all around. If a place exists, it stands to reason that you must be able, somehow, to reach it from wherever you are.

New ways of conveying meaning should always be welcome in our personal growth plan. We should look for shades of meaning when people address us in a certain way. Think about the person who inquires "How are you *really?*" The tone implies that you are a chronic complainer who likes to drop a list of ailments or emotional upsets on the ears of the questioner.

Some word symbols have greater potency than others when used to describe people's character. For instance, if we hear the words lawyer, husband, Oriental, and athlete used to describe a person, we will remember the word "Oriental" as the strongest description of the total person. If the descriptive words scholar, author, consultant, and divorced are used to indicate a certain person, "divorced" is the label we are likely to remember. This is because our society places great emphasis on conformity. Both Oriental and divorced stand apart from the mainstream of American life.

Certain words that we use in everyday talk are rife with personal indictments of others. Consider how often we hear the labels "neurotic" or "paranoid" attached to perfectly innocent victims. We can dismiss whole personalities as incompetent, maladjusted, or perverted simply because they look the part of the emotionally loaded labels that are affixed to them.

Take a look at the labels that people assign to themselves. There aren't any more "janitors" around buildings. They have all become "custodial engineers." "Maids" are out; "domestic consultants" are in. Few people feel secure about identifying themselves with the proper job title. The race to be on top of the pack has pushed egos to claim titles they don't hold. Why do we tend to be apologetic about our rank-and-file occupation? If we are a floorwalker in a department store, why must we insist upon the title "aisle manager" when we describe our job? Supposedly it is better for our image to be a manager than a walker. In the same vein, "tree trimmers" have become "tree surgeons" because surgeon sounds more prestigious than trimmer.

With the competition for jobs so fierce, the desire to paint our wagons in colors we *wish* we had can be overwhelming. Lately, it seems that monologues of this sort abound around every corner:

> Well, the president of the company has interviewed over three hundred people for the job and he has finally narrowed it down to three. Of course, with my background and experience, I was automatically chosen as one of the finalists. There's a good chance that I'll head the company some day.

How many times do we hear people say that they were one out of six or seven hundred chosen for a "top" management job? No one admits to being picked for a "middle" management position, and the "bottom" slot has been eliminated entirely. Where there used to be a single dean in charge of a college program of studies, there are now several deans, all vying for top billing. How refreshing it must be to hear a cobbler say that he is a *good* cobbler, not a "shoe surgeon" or "shoe redesigner."

Because we are ever-changing in our perceptions and attitudes toward events, it is wise to keep a close watch on the words we use to describe ourselves, our views of things past and to come, and our occupational status. If we can be literally honest about who we are and where we stand in the scheme of things, we will realize that greater satisfaction can be had through being a local journalist or writer for the daily newspaper than through tooting the horn of "investigative reporter" for all to be awed by. All reporting is investigative, and all journalism is investigative. In fact, any position we will ever occupy has its "investigative" dimension. It simply means that we have done our homework by looking up information we need to do the job. By the same token, why have "action news"? All news is action, but not all action is news.

If the concept of "nightly news" has lost its luster, why not have a rock band play right through the headlines and the more serious stories? Then we'd have "disco-action-news," and who knows where that would end? Weather reports have also been glamorized. We have "accu-weather," which is supposed to suggest the accuracy of a report that, by its very nature, can never be accurate.

The Admen

The language of advertising requires word-watching of the closest sort. Because we are cajoled and pushed and jollied into purchasing so many items we don't need, we can say that the media people have done an admirable job of selling over the air waves and in print.

Consider the ad in the local newspaper offering the position of Distinguished Professor. Since "professor" no longer seems to be enough of a recommendation to the post of teacher of higher learning, how does one mark the difference between a Distinguished and an Ordinary Professor? What would an Undistinguished Professor look like? Perhaps he'd be in his mid-twenties, carry his books in a brown paper bag, and wear sneakers and chinos.

Observe the headlines in the daily newspapers. One headline recently announced: "Dynamic Blonde Fatally Shot." How does one know that the victim was dynamic, or all that blonde? What if the victim were less vivacious and less blonde? Would it lessen the crime any? Because we reject adjectives that connote plainness, even mildly attractive victims are labeled "beautiful," and more attractive ones are "dazzling," "gorgeous," "sensational."

"Sensational" is also the label frequently affixed to films by critics when all other adjectives fail. With any thought on the matter, "sensational" simply means anything that applies or relates to the senses. Since all movies do that, it is the very heart of the nature of film. The critical question is how *well* does the film appeal to the senses? When critics over-praise the common feature film with blurbs like "Fantastic!" "Super!" "A Maximum Experience!" are they really saying "A Routine Experience," "Can't Get That Excited About It," and "An Adequate Performance"?

If all the superlatives are heaped upon the adequate cultural experiences, what words are left to describe the truly outstanding, brilliant, totally absorbing, if rare, masterworks? Recently, we have been duped into thinking that because a particular film is successful, an endless road of sequels will be just as enticing. Witness the plethora of I, II, and III movies, such as *The Godfather, Jaws, Rocky,* and *Superman.*

As for television commercials, more damage is done to our psyches than we care to admit. We are, in fact, reduced to babbling idiots who can't discriminate between necessities and luxuries. What is done to the remnants of our dignity via the air waves is nothing short of a numbing of the senses, a belittling of the intellect. Analyze the effects of the language of advertising upon the emotions. Consider the following appeals to public taste:

1. How can a carbonated beverage, for example, taste like love? Love is a complicated emotion that couldn't possibly be compared with the taste of a soda, carbonated or not. To elevate soda to the level of the most powerful emotion known to mankind is to reduce the importance of love to the fizzle and impermanence of the drink.

2. If "you're where you want to be, because your soda is sugar-free," you should evaluate where you really are in terms of life goals. If you want to be where you are at present, it is not through the merits of your soda-pop.

3. "I don't believe I ate the whole thing" is, of course, an ad for the overeater. To "eat the whole thing" is a vulgar display of rapid food ingestion. It also assumes that such an extreme condition can be remedied by dropping a few tablets into a glass of water. This act will supposedly fizzle you down to normal size.

4. The selling of detergents is one of the more obvious efforts of the admen to cater to subnormal intelligences. Supposedly, we are a dismally unhappy people unless our whites are whiter and our brights brighter. Why the need to sell soap at all? We would buy it anyway.

5. What we usually think of as news is bad news. Good news doesn't make good copy. It isn't violent or sensational enough. Commercials must dig into the recesses of the consciousness and portray those images which make us react strongly and favorably to what is being sold. What terrible shape our house would be in if we didn't use this kind of paint. Your neighbors will surely shun you if you care for your

lawn yourself instead of summoning a "professional." No one should speak to you unless you use a certain toothpaste. And you won't have any dates, either.

Be aware of the power that advertising wields over you. It plays to your weaknesses and inadequacies. It shows you the poor housewife who fails miserably at her daily tasks until she uses a floor-polish that doesn't coat with waxy build-up. Under the thumb of the adpeople, even your social lives and friendships are up for questioning. Will your friends ever visit you again if you don't serve them mountain-grown coffee? Remember, all coffee is mountain-grown, just as all news is action news. Next time around, listen hard when a salesman tells you, in a minute of television time, to run out to buy a Gusto car because nine out of every ten Gustos bought in the last ten years are still on the road today. When you consider that many Gustos may be on the *side* of the road or up on cement blocks, the ad loses impact. Also, is a "pre-owned" Gusto any better than a secondhand one?

Watch the words that manipulate or coerce you into doing the things you do, or that make you inert enough to refuse the name of action. The next time your loved one complains of an unsightly ring around his collar, advise him to wash his neck. It removes dirt instantly and extends the life of the shirt. Ask yourself, too, if you really need the "world's smartest camera." After all, if a camera is more knowledgeable than a human being, we are all in serious straits.

Know when you've been hoodwinked by word-tricks. If you're a shrewd word-watcher, you won't be taken in.

Watching Political Words

What makes you vote for the candidate of your choice? Most likely it is the words he chooses to say and the promises he makes on the campaign trail. When Richard Nixon voiced his ubiquitous phrase, "Let me make one thing perfectly clear," he immediately made unclear what he professed to clarify. Politicians are not the only professionals who garble and obscure what should be essentially clear concepts, but they are in the public eye more than other professional people. Common expressions like the ones that follow should give some idea of the sound, not the sense, that our phrase-makers invent.

Expression	*Meaning*
You opened a whole can of worms.	Listen, I wish I knew the answer. I'll stall with some general, obscure expressions, and maybe you—and your question—will go away.
détente	Anything anyone wants it to mean. It vaguely has something to do with getting along with other nations. It sounds impressive.
in the field	You are creatively unavailable to appear for an appointment. It could mean anything from being on the beach to being out to lunch. Occasionally, it signals involvement in a worthwhile activity.
controversial	Anything that can't be solved right away.
pacification	Sometimes innocent lives are lost during time of war.
"—gate," as in Watergate or Koreagate	A political movement or event of suspicious nature, alien to the integrity of the democratic process.
antipersonnel	The enemy.
In point of fact, it is not an unfounded assumption to say that . . .	I think.
We are concerned that you receive a quality education.	"Quality" needs a modifier, an adjective. A "quality" education can be of poor quality.
ball-park figure	The figure quoted will be higher when it is passed on to the consumer.

From the final days of the Nixon administration came a barrage of fuzzy words, all sounding equally mysterious and obscure: stonewalling, synergizing, railroading. The continual modification of congressional jargon is designed to avoid precise definition. The committees of congress were recently assigned the new label of "work groups" or "study groups," because the traditional concept of "committee" implied endless stalling and little work done. The political "system" has become the political "community" because "system" is a harsh word. "Community"

has a warmth about it, implying that the people within it truly care for one another in selfless, noncompetitive ways. It falls more easily on the ears.

The words cited above have been repeated so often that we are still buried under the delusions they generated. Politicians in general are accused of offering standard evasive replies that appear to sound enlightening at first, but on second hearing don't hold up. A good listener can tell the difference right away.

Watching Legal Words

The jargon of the legal profession has always been easy to hide behind. If you examine certain legal expressions for clarity and plain sense, you will be disappointed. Clarity can be shrouded in multiple, meaningless words. Overlong sentences are employed to state simple ideas. The query "What did he say?" is often put to those in the legal profession. Here are just a few examples of the dilemma:

Instead of	*Use*
I will make substantial and effective inquiry into . . .	I will ask . . .
He is fully cognizant and consciously aware. . . .	He knows . . .
The extension of coverage to include all employees, regardless of length of service to the company and meritorious performance, does not appear to be as feasible as the initial surveys indicated.	Not all employees will be covered by the new policy.

We have watched other people's words in the first part of this chapter. The remainder of the chapter will be devoted to watching our own words.

Word-Watching for Fun and Profit

We have seen how various words have taken on different meanings in the course of time. A look at our changing language should encourage us to know the infinite variety of meanings that are attached to many words in an everyday context. If we can be clear about what we mean to say, and then say it, we should have no trouble in being understood. Because we change so rapidly in our acquisition of new knowledge, new facts, new opinions, it is a good thing to see our words as expressions of our self-ness. Our language should come to *mean* or express the total impact of ourselves upon others. What the ad agencies tell us and the lawyers and politicians communicate to us should be quickly evaluated for substance and meaning. The important thing for us to remember is that when we don't understand what is being said to us, it is the fault of the speaker for not making the words clear, not that of the listener for failing to understand.

Our words should be watched with care if we intend to make the most of our natural talents. We need to exercise our spoken skills until they do for us all that they can. Practice notes of many kinds should make up our working library. If we watch our own words carefully, we will have eliminated at least half the difficulties that two people encounter when they attempt to communicate.

In the pages that follow, all kinds of words will be offered to you for practice. Most of them are everyday words that many of us mispronounce. Others are less common words, but they provide good examples of how the lips, teeth, tongue, and jaw should work together in order to produce the best sound. What follows is a mini-laboratory of all kinds of sounds and sense. Add to these your own "pet peeve" words and practice them along with words you find difficult to say. Feel free to consult the most popular dictionaries for additional help with pronunciation. These include Webster's *New World Dictionary of the American Language, The American College Dictionary,* and Webster's *New International Dictionary.* Kenyon and Knott's *A Pronouncing Dictionary of American English* is also helpful.

Consonant substitutions are common in these words:

absorb	seven	length	newspaper	chimney
absurd	eleven	strength	architect	letter
pumpkin	naphtha	gesture	tremendous	
pantomime	diphtheria	chasm	trough	

a. doing, coming, going, working, morning. Avoid substituting *n* for *ng*.
b. notice, kitty, metal, party, later, water, tattle, little, battle. Avoid substituting *d* for *t* between vowels.
c. where, what, which, why, when. Avoid substituting *w* for *wh*.
d. bird, word, learn, curl, serve. Avoid substituting *oi* for the stressed syllable *r*.
e. then, them, the, this, those. Avoid substituting *d* for *th*.
f. garage, rouge, camouflage, mirage, prestige. Avoid substituting *j* for *zh* at the ends of words.

Vowel substitutions are common in these words:

get	had	can	alias	wander
instead	began	such	genuine	penalize
again	just	I'll	theater	demeanor
every	sure	I'm	piano	guarantee
guess	your	our	wrestle	complacent
together	poor	milk	deaf	consul
catch	fire	soot	ate	era

Reversals of sounds or syllables are common in these words:

pretty	prepare	provide	aggravate
children	professor	introduce	geography
hundred	produce	reproduce	perform
brethren	protect	represent	calvary
modern	aluminum	perspiration	cavalry

Omissions of sounds or syllables are common in these words:

usual	perhaps	diamond	temperature	gentlemen
mutual	suppose	diary	arctic	help
casual	surprised	violent	adjective	picture
believe	suspenders	medieval	asked	government
belong	company	beauteous	candidate	environment
escape	personal	geography	understand	recognize
eleven	police	probably	friendly	poem

a. last, next, must, past, best. Avoid omitting *t* when it is final.
b. kept, wept, slept, crept. Avoid omitting *t* after *p*.
c. didn't, couldn't, hadn't, shouldn't, wouldn't. Avoid omitting *t* in contractions.
d. figure, mercury, regular. Avoid omitting medial *u* after *g* or *c* in words like these.
e. human, huge, humanity, hue. Avoid omitting *h* before *u*.

Misplaced stress is a common error in these words:

baptize	receipt	routine	horizon
chastise	relapse	impotent	component
divorce	secrete	influence	explosive
dissect	eclipse	mischievous	ascertain
default	hotel	theater	hospitable
decoy	insane	vehement	comparable

Vowel substitutions are common in these classes of words:

a. until, unless, unable, unload, undo. Avoid substituting *a* for *u* in "un" syllables.
b. soda, sofa, camera, Alabama, China. Avoid saying "sody," etc.
c. dishes, fishes, wishes, collision, division. Give full "sh" sound.
d. ink, think, sink, drink. Avoid substituting *e* for *i* before nk.
e. egg, leg, peg, keg. Avoid substituting *a* for *e* before g.
f. measure, pleasure, treasure, special, pressure, fresh. Avoid substituting *a* for *e* before *s* or *sh.*
g. ten, men, engine, kettle, head. Avoid substituting *i* for *e* before n, t, or d, especially before n.
h. farm, part, park, barn, card. Avoid substituting *o* for *a* before r.
i. fellow, window, yellow, potato, tomato. Avoid saying "fella," etc.
j. bushes, push, cushion, bushel. Avoid substituting *oo* for *u* before sh.
k. town, out, cow, down, house. Avoid substituting *au* for *ou.*
l. boil, point, poison, boisterous. Avoid substituting *er* for *oi.*
m. coil, oily, choice, voice. Avoid substituting *er* for *oi.*

Additions of sounds or syllables are common in these words:

attacked	villain	toward	wash	elm
drowned	municipal	calm	across	cruelty
coupon	statistics	almond	athlete	frailty
column	overalls	subtle	umbrella	grievous
columnist	height	epistle	arithmetic	barbarous
percolator	forehead	corps	remnant	accompanist

Points to be remembered:

1. Do not omit unaccented syllables in such words as *history* (histry), *arithmetic* (rithmetic), *boisterous* (boistrous), *interest* (intrest), *valuable* (valuble), *victory* (victry).
2. Do not say *unt* in such words as government, document, prudent.
3. Do not say *id* for *ed* in such words as delighted, excited, united.
4. Do not say *in* for *ing* in such words as singing, reading, writing.
5. Do not say *unce* for *ence* in such words as sentence, patience, experience.
6. Be sure to sound the *d,* when preceded by *n,* in such words as *stand* (stan), *depends* (depens), *grandfather* (granfather), *handful* (hanful).
7. Be sure to sound the *h* in such words as which, when, white, shrill, shrine, shrub.

Compare ng with n endings:

taking—taken	eating—eaten	rotting—rotten
sodding—sodden	bearing—barren	seizing—season
guarding—garden	ribbing—ribbon	balding—bacon
butting—button	canning—cannon	

Sounds and stresses:

Initial	*Medial*	*Final*
day	didn't	add
dear	couldn't	aid
did	hadn't	bed
dog	shouldn't	could

Initial	*Medial*	*Final*
door	hidden	food
down	ready	good
paper	apple	camp
party	apron	help
pull	pepper	stop
pack	report	up
pin	separate	rope
back	about	crib
barn	anybody	grab
basket	baby	knob
bear	fable	rob
before	table	web
came	biscuit	book
car	making	look
garden	again	beg
value	cover	above
variety	driver	believe
visit	over	glove
thank	author	bath
think	birthday	cloth
three	something	mouth
threw	southward	north
they	mother	soothe
shade	addition	brush
shall	bushel	cash
know	any	again
nest	only	can
must	coming	home
made	farmer	same
may	famous	time
chain	butcher	beach
chalk	kitchen	bunch
chew	merchant	much
eagle	green	flee
alive	parasol	polka
table	notice	about

The next few exercises will give you practice in putting isolated sounds and words into various contexts. The first of these vocal workouts offers help in phrasing, grouping of ideas, rhythm, cadence, articulation, and emphasis of key words and phrases. Say each sentence with the intention of extracting from it the greatest possible meaning.

1. A tedious person is one a man would leap a steeple from, gallop down any steep hill to avoid.   (Ben Jonson)
2. What the reason of an ant laboriously drags into a heap, the wind of accident will collect in one breath.   (Schiller)
3. If a man will begin with certainties, he will end with doubts; but if he will be content to begin with doubts, he shall end in certainties.
                                                           (Francis Bacon)
4. In great straits and when hope is small, the boldest counsels are the safest.   (Livy)
5. Of all villainy, there is none so base as the hypocrite, who, at the moment he is most false, takes care to appear most virtuous.
                                                              (Cicero)
6. He who is false to present duty breaks a thread in the loom, and will find the flaw when he may have forgotten its cause.
                                                       (Henry W. Beecher)

Here is an exercise in combining sound and non-sense with the sense you can make of the overall piece. It is a poem by Lewis Carroll entitled "Jabberwocky." You can *hear* meanings if you listen while you talk it out.

> 'Twas brillig, and the slithy toves
>   Did gyre and gimble in the wabe:
> All mimsy were the borogoves,
>   And the mome raths outgrabe.
>
> "Beware the Jabberwock, my son!
>   The jaws that bite, the claws that catch!
> Beware the jubjub bird, and shun
>   The frumious Bandersnatch!"

He took his vorpal sword in hand:
Long time the manxome foe he sought—
So rested he by the Tumtum tree,
And stood awhile in thought.

And, as in uffish thought he stood,
The Jabberwock, with eyes of flame,
Came whiffling through the tulgey wood.
And burbled as it came!

One, two! One, two! And through and through
The vorpal blade went snicker-snack!
He left it dead, and with its head
He went galumphing back.

"And hast thou slain the Jabberwock?
Come to my arms, my beamish boy!
O frabjous day! Calloh, Callay!"
He chortled in his joy.

'Twas brillig, and the slithy toves
Did gyre and gimble in the wabe:
All mimsy were the borogoves,
And the mome raths outgrabe.

You can easily invent meanings for these strange sounds. Perhaps "bril-lig" could be a combination of "brilliant" and "frigid." "Slithy" sounds a bit like a cross between "slippery" and "steathily." Is "mimsy" a compound of "flimsy" and "whimsical?" You are right about the inter-pretations you insist upon. Whatever meanings you can guess at, the poem is a wonderful one for polishing your sounds and hearing yourself sharpen each syllable.

Mark Twain, the great American humorist and chronicler, had a special gift for making pictures with words. He *felt* detail the way we *see* it. This excerpt from *Life on the Mississippi* provides many good words in good order to be spoken well. Say each word carefully in your mind. Enter the words into proper phrases. Stretch the phrases into colorful sentences, and you have a polished piece to practice with.

When I was a boy, there was but one permanent ambition among my comrades in our village on the west bank of the Mississippi River. That was to be a steamboatman. We had transient ambitions of other sorts, but they were only transient. When a circus came and went, it left us all burning to become clowns; the first Negro minstrel show that ever came to our section left us all suffering to try that kind of life; now and then we had a hope that if we lived and we were good, God would permit us to be pirates. These ambitions faded out each in its turn, but the ambition to be a steamboatman always remained.

Once a day a cheap, gaudy packet arrived upward from St. Louis, and another downward from Keokuk. Before these events, the day was glorious with expectancy; after them, the day was a dead and empty thing. Not only the boys but the whole village felt this. After all these years I can picture that old time to myself now, just as it was then; the white town drowsing in the sunshine of a summer's morning; the streets empty, or pretty nearly so; one or two clerks sitting in front of the Water Street stores, with their splint-bottomed chairs tilted back against the walls, asleep with shingle shavings enough around to show what broke them down . . .

The content of this chapter should be only the beginning of word-watching for you. It is an art that can lift you from the commonplace to the extraordinary. There are always enough words to choose from that are simple, direct, and mean just what you want them to mean. You don't need a fancy vocabulary to be verbally well dressed. All you need to move ahead is the right word, in the right order, at the right time.

CHAPTER V

Talk Your Way to Success

Our doubts are traitors,
And make us lose the good we oft might win
By fearing to attempt.

—Shakespeare

In its broadest and best sense, all good talk is persuasion of some sort. Most of the time you are, by your words, persuading others to like you better or believe in you a little more. You are constantly in the process of selling yourself: your ideas, talents, capabilities, ability to work well with others. On your way up the ladder of success, you have only your words and your deeds to tell anyone about you. Of these two instruments of evaluation, actions that are not supported or defended by words, or words unaccompanied by appropriate action, seem to be incomplete gestures of a single act. For instance, if an extremely shy person accomplishes a great undertaking for the company or the group he works with, but lacks the words to say how he did it or why, he is in the same class as one who is known for inaction. Braggarts, after all, talk about what they *didn't* do. If you can't talk about what you *did* do, what was the sense of doing it in the first place? Not talking will not move you ahead. To do something "above and beyond the call of duty" is a wonderful thing. To explain or describe it accurately is even better. It shows that you know what you're doing and where you want to go. It is not always true that actions speak louder than words. Usually the two speak together. If you do those things you say you believe in, your words and actions have some relationship to each other. There is a consistency in them that identifies you as a person of character who can be relied upon to see things through.

Face-to-face communication seems to be the best method of selling yourself. There are other ways, to be sure, but they seem to be less effective than the instantly conveyed personal-appearance message. Letter-writing or memo-jotting gets things done, but it is more difficult to sell your total self through the mail or over the telephone. The mail can't supply all the human detail that is available in face-to-face encounters. When you talk yourself into being understood by others, it is probably because your body-language, eye-touch, and gestures combine with your words to form an appealing visual and verbal picture. It has been established that the officials of most successful enterprises communicate frequently with their employees on a face-to-face basis, rather than through media channels or messengers. It is impossible to respond to a memo in the same way that you react to a living being who stands a foot and a half away from you.

Close Encounters of the Best Kind

A primary requirement for success in the art of talking is never to speak without relating what is being said to the persons listening. To talk in a vacuum, without tying the speaker and hearer together in an intellectual or emotional bond—or both—is a futile exercise in communication. You might as well talk to yourself, which is a worthwhile project of another sort.

When you talk to yourself, you have the advantage of believing and understanding your own thoughts without effort. You don't need to clarify them or outline motives. You have an instant sympathizer and friend in yourself. You can take all kinds of verbal shortcuts when you speak to your mind. For one thing, you can think five times faster than you can talk. You don't need words for the thinking process. You need symbols, and those you have by the thousands. The next time you stop in your car for a red light, observe the driver in the lane next to you. If the driver is alone, sometimes you can catch him in the act of communicating with himself. His eyebrows may be raised or furrowed. He may scratch his head in bewilderment, or tug at his ears. At the same time you may see his mouth moving. The corners of the mouth may be turned up in a smile or down in a frown. These nonverbal gestures indicate that the person is having a chat with himself. He is in the process of straightening something out or thinking something through.

While a certain amount of self-talk is necessary, total absorption in this activity can cut you off from the vital mainstream of human interaction. The most productive kinds of encounters, however, occur *after* you have spoken with yourself. You know where you stand on certain issues, and you're ready for a full and frank exchange of ideas. There are many kinds of talk-situations that can help you to shine in your own right. The most popular of these is conversation.

Conversation usually occurs between two people, but more can join in if the climate is right. Such talk is usually of a general nature, dealing with topics like current issues or the best place to spend your vacation. Being able to talk well in conversation makes your presence greatly desired at any kind of social gathering, formal or informal. People will want to be around you when you converse if:

You know the art of asking the right questions. These questions should be able to draw shy people out of themselves and make them eager to respond to you. Be careful not to repeat trite questions about the weather or irreversible calamities. Such inquiries are plainly uninteresting, and they can be answered with a flat word or two. "Nice day?" "Yes." The expert conversationalist recognizes the question that must be acknowledged with at least a few sentences. Rather than "Do you play baseball?", which can be answered with a "yes" or "no," how about "Which sports are you especially active in or interested in?" This gives your partner a chance to reflect on what is meaningful to him. It also puts you in first place by showing an interest in other people.

> Judge a man by the questions he asks.
>
> —Voltaire

You perceive everyone as having more knowledge than you. While this may not be entirely true, you stand to learn much through conversing with all kinds and levels of people. At a cocktail party, for instance, there are always a few guests who talk only of those who have "big names," or who are worth "being seen with." Remember, the truly magnificent human being treats with kindness and courtesy someone who can be of no possible service to him. Although most people may not know more than you, they know *different* things, things that you never took the time to learn. Everyone can tell us something we didn't know before. Even children, with their simple, unsophisticated language, can show us a truth or an idea that never occurred to us before.

You listen with the curiosity of a child. To infants, everything is interesting. As we grow older, fewer things are as attractive as they once were. We have to learn all over again to pull ourselves up by the hair, turn ourselves inside out, and see the world with fresh eyes. Be careful

"As I Was Saying . . ."

of labeling everything "boring." If you do, you risk falling victim to your own boredom. A vast emptiness can set in when you think this way. If you look upon every moment as a time to be filled with a new adventure, you will be vital and dynamic in your own right. Your eyes will sparkle, and your words won't be laden with a "What's good about it?" philosophy. Instead, you will find that listening to the accounts of others' lives can be quite delightful after all. For one thing, others will enjoy your company enormously. For another, listening to them keeps you from falling into the "I" syndrome. After a while,

the "I" people don't find themselves invited back to many conversations.
Here is a checklist of things to avoid when you are trying to make
good conversation.

a. Talking only about subjects that interest you.
b. Talking about yourself in terms of successes or achievements only.
c. Gossiping.
d. Interrupting others with lines like "I know how that story ends."
e. Arguing.
f. Asking embarrassing personal questions.
g. Destroying the atmosphere for good conversation. You can do
   this by abruptly leaving your partner for no good reason, by turning your head away, or by going off to refresh a drink. You can
   turn others off by yawning visibly or audibly, and by looking at
   your watch while others are talking.

Another type of conversation is the interview. It has a purpose of
its own and is generally more serious than everyday converstion. The
interview has to do with the gathering and dispensing of information
needed to accomplish a certain goal. One kind of interview provides
information that illuminates another person's life. An example of this
type of encounter is when a television talk-show host questions guests

William Henry Harbinger

about their latest book, or their philosophy of life, or the elements that make for a successful career. Notice the kinds of questions that are asked. They are of a general nature in the beginning, or warm-up, then usually proceed to the specific and finally to the personal and even the sensational.

The job interview is more serious in intent than the media interview. Although job interviews may sound casual and conversational, there is always an implicit goal. Both parties know this, and they must continue to move toward the expected outcome or resolution. A few hints for helping the interview to come off well, at least in terms of talk, are the following:

1. Be aware that the person interviewing you can only know what you choose to tell him about yourself. Choose, then, to say your words carefully. Words about you and from you should highlight your strengths without exaggeration, and downplay your weaknesses.

2. Don't make the interviewer do all the work. If he has to ask you twenty-one questions, and you answer them all with a "yes" or a "no," you're not doing any work on your own behalf. Show that you know something about the company and say what you can do for them. Make them feel that they need your special skills and abilities.

3. Don't come right out and ask for the job. Ask, rather, if your interviewer might be willing to circulate your credentials to other potential employers who need skills similar to yours. This is a nice way of not putting your interviewer on the spot. You can make more friends and build more contacts by simply discussing your future than you can by showing a desperate need for a particular job.

4. Know by name a key person in the company you want to work for. If you send a résumé and cover letter to a vague title such as Director of Office Personnel, your communication may be "misplaced" in record time.

5. Jobs are had or lost in the first three minutes of the interview. Your opening remarks are all-important. They should show a positive, sincere, optimistic expression of yourself. In your mind should be the words: "They are lucky to have me work for them."

6. Try to make people remember you. Say something a bit out of the ordinary. Shake hands a little more firmly than the person before

or after you. Have a stronger eye-touch or a bit more confidence than
you had for the last job interview. Know more by having read more.
Be able to talk on a wide variety of subjects.

7. Remember that success in any field of endeavor depends more

"I'm So Glad We've Had This Little Discussion."

on energy and drive than it does on intelligence. To work hard is the
sincerest compliment to your personal growth.

Another type of talk-situation is the group discussion. This is a common way of communicating on the job. Talking in a group requires
different skills, but no less energies, than does talking one-to-one as
in a conversation. While one or two people independently can make
decisions *faster* than three or more people in a group, it is believed
by many communication analysts that group decisions are the *better*
in quality. Group discussions are what became of "meetings," which
were gatherings of people to address problems they couldn't handle
alone. If the members of a group talk well, each with the others, it
usually means that they have done their share of homework. There
are study groups, social groups, religious groups, political groups, educa-

tional groups, management groups, labor groups. What they have in common is that they are all problem-solving groups; that is, the people meet to settle issues of concern to them. The nature of group work is interdependence. If someone comes to the group unprepared to contribute his or her ideas, the whole group suffers a setback. Each member should, ideally, research a different aspect of a problem for the best outcome of the discussion. Some hindrances to productive group talk are:

1. A vague statement of an unclear problem. If the group doesn't know *exactly* what the problem is, a solution is impossible. The important thing to remember in group-talk is that nothing much gets done after the first half hour. People become restless, the problem appears more obscure, and the solution more improbable than ever.

2. Neglecting to pinpoint probable causes of the problem. Once a problem is located and defined, a cause for it should be examined. Keep in mind that all good problem-solving is done through collective action and cooperation by the group members. Many minds shed a brighter light on a larger issue. Discussion is an ideal form of democracy.

3. Neglecting to arrive at several possible solutions. If each member of the group proposed one studied resolution to the group's dilemma, there would be many creative avenues of approach to the problem. Bear in mind, though, that many problems have no answers, even after careful study and deliberation. If you find this to be the case, be content with simply exposing the problem.

4. Failing to list the advantages and disadvantages of every proposed resolution. This includes presentation of objective evidence, not just offhand opinion or educated guesses.

5. Neglecting to put the best solution into effect. This final step in the group process should be the easiest to carry out. The hard work has been done, and the solution agreed upon. Implementing it may call for the formation of another group or "task force."

Group-talk operates most successfully when all the members are willing to discuss their common problems openly. The group works best when it is small enough for everyone to have equal time. All the members should be equally prepared and capable of the particular kind of thinking that is involved in their project. For example, a social group that meets to decide where and when to hold its next fund-raiser doesn't need the close, critical kind of thinking that national policy-makers need when they review the draft laws.

Effective discussion serves to unite groups and adds an atmosphere of fellowship to an institution or organization. It allows for expression of different points of view and encourages separate and combined study of a common concern. Moreover, a number of fresh ideas, which would never be heard in private decision-making processes, are allowed to be shared. The result should be a richer, well-rounded experience for all.

How much talk is expected of each group member? The amount of talk one does is not as important as the quality of what is said. Some people talk nonstop and say nothing. Others may not speak for a long time, then say something startling or enlightening. As with all groups, the leader or moderator must take the reins or the horse will gallop away. The leader is responsible for calming the anxious talker and encouraging the quiet one. The leader should be more than a successful talker. He or she must be an effective listener. He listens for when the discussion gets off the track and runs loose, for when it moves along, and for when it must stop. He tactfully suppresses the monopolizer by giving others the chance to be heard.

What kind of talk is most effective when dealing with groups? The best way to be readily understood is to repeat the basic ideas of the speaker who precedes you. For example, the last person to talk had a specific message to get across. Perhaps it had to do with the number of paid vacation days the company gives. To clarify his words in your mind, you should say, "Bill, do I understand you to say that the company needs a new policy on the matter of paid vacation days?" If Bill answers "yes" to your question, you can go on from there. If "no," then find out what he meant before you can respond properly. Dealing with words in this way is a slower process than we are used to, but it is virtually error-free.

Another type of talk-situation is the more formal lecture-discussion format, where you as talker come prepared to do most of the work. The burden of leadership falls on you. You command the absolute attention of the group. It is your chance to be seen and heard. It may well be your chance to move ahead. When you do this kind of talking, you are saying that you can handle responsibility. You are also implying that leadership roles are what you are after, and you don't mind the tensions that this kind of talk generates. It is your way of showing belief in yourself.

When you talk "solo," that is, not within the group structure, you are in charge of the space around you. If you have prepared well for this moment, you have nothing to worry about. Remember these three simple rules, and you can guarantee yourself a job well done.

1. Tell your listeners what you are going to say.
2. Say it.
3. Tell your listeners what you just said.

Notice that the beginning and the conclusion introduce and summarize the main point of your talk. Everything else in the middle is supporting dialogue or evidence. The outline of your words should look like a hammock, where the two ends are planted solidly in the ground, and the middle has a bit more freedom to move. Like a good hammock, the middle of your talk shouldn't sag too much or you won't be comfortable. The "sag" should be used wisely. It can be made tight or loose, depending on your listeners' response.

You as talker should always be conscious of the big idea you want to get across. The language you choose should have its roots in the common parlance of your listeners. For example, if you are a government official and you are talking to members of your staff, you can use complex terminology because the staff is familiar with it. If you talk about the processes of government to a group of high-school sophomores, you must select other kinds of words to communicate your big idea. Your message should be organized in such a way that it seems logical for you to proceed as you do from one thought to another. When listeners become restless, they are responding to a lack of order in your words. We are born with a desire for some kind of order in our lives. When we criticize a sculpture, a painting, a dance, it is because we detect a lack of order somewhere within it. Even when we are being entertained by a frivolous story, the storyteller has to begin at the beginning and end at the end.

Your talk should have built-in order. If you need gestures or visual aids to bring this order into sharper focus, use them. Know why your listeners have come to hear you. Send your message to them clearly, using all the inner energies you can muster. Next to order, energy is the most valuable asset that a talker can have. Energy doesn't have to be shown by leaping around the room or by shouting. It is that inner dynamism, that glow by which people are transformed in your presence, and you in their presence. Energy has to do with the eyes, the shoulders, the hands and feet. In other words, if you can talk "from the ankles up," you will be energetic and vital enough to be remembered. A sluggish body conveys its own message. It says to its hearers, "Don't bother me. I was out late last night. It's very hard for me to move. I'll just sit here at the edge of the table and hang on." The trick with good talking is to *deny* that you are exhausted, or bothered by some problem, or plumb out of energy. If you tell your body that you need it for this talk, it will be your friend and come with you.

How do you know what all those eyes and ears out there think about you as you talk your way to success? You must depend on the hidden signals of the feedback process to supply this information. These messages are often nonverbal. A nod of the head, a hand raised to ask a question, a smile or glance of approval: those signals indicate that you are being received well. On the other hand, if your listeners take out their handkerchiefs to mop their brows on a hot summer afternoon, it indicates that they are more aware of the heat than of your presence. The successful talker makes people forget any unpleasant distractions and focus their attention on him.

How can you keep your listeners glued to you? The best way is to say familiar ideas in unusual language. Choose your words as if you shopped for them in the finest stores. Here is an example of the power of words in an ordinary setting:

There was a man who owned a small company. He was very good to his employees. They confided in him and considered him their father. One of his workers left him and was out of work for some time. The worker's dearest possession was his little son, whom he proudly carried about with him. One day, despondent as he was, he packed up his little son and went to visit his old boss. The worker was absorbed in his gloom when he said to his boss, "Look how bad things are. I have a son and no job." The kindly boss took him by the arm and responded: "Look how bad things are. I have a job and no son." From then on, the man with the young son was a different person. He was changed because of *words* that were spoken to him. They are powerful enough to turn whole lives around.

To sharpen your wits with regard to words well spoken and quickly invented, play a few practice games. Select a group of friends to help you. Assign them parts to play as members of your practice audience. You'll need: (1) a heckler, (2) someone who offers only negative feedback, (3) a curious and interested listener, and (4) someone who talks to other members of the audience while you are talking. See if you can find ways to deal with these kinds of listeners. You need to consider your own talk-style in order to determine new approaches for handling various levels of audience interest. If you believe in yourself enough, you can take on the heckler and come out a winner. Dealing with hostile listeners demands all of your mettle and wit. One way to acknowledge hostility is to confront it directly. If you can befriend your heckler or constant interrupter in some way, you have won a convert, which is more challenging than retaining a friend. You can usually win over hostile faces by picking up first on body cues, then on explicit verbal outbursts. A person who sits with arms folded tightly, with rigid body, is likely to be an angry listener. Be alert to a possible confrontation. When it comes, you can handle it by appealing to his sympathy. You can calmly respond with such remarks as "I agree with you," or "What would it take to convince you that . . . ?" The latter question puts the ball into the angry person's court. He must respond to your question now. This method of calling upon your listeners also gives you the time to catch your breath and think.

You can practice with your game audience in many other ways. Practice helps you to anticipate the worst but hope for the best. Ask your friends to serve as an audience and sit with their backs to you as you talk. This is a different test of your ingenuity. You can also ask your friends to sit facing you with paper bags or hoods over their heads. This arrangement will show you how difficult it is to speak without response or feedback. It will make you appreciate how alive your listeners can be in a normal setting.

Prove It

When you set out to sell yourself through talk, you need to know something about the art of persuasion and how it works. In its best sense, persuasion is any attempt to change another's mind or to reinforce what he already believes to be true. If you know that you aren't getting on with your employer or with someone whom you really need on

"There's No Arguing With Angelico."

your side, you must change that person's opinion of you. If, on the other hand, you have a good friend who backs you on your way to success, you need to solidify or reinforce that relationship from time to time if it is to maintain its value.

You enhance your credibility when you are able to prove that your statements are true. Proof can be had in many ways. You can prove anything you say if you have evidence, statistics, or testimony. If you have evidence, you have compiled enough hard facts to warrant belief. For example, if you are proving that you have the experience needed to qualify for a certain job, you should be able to produce evidence of such qualifications. This evidence may take the form of letters from your previous employers, or a personal file of documented material that would enable anyone to see at a glance that you are what you say you are. Statistics usually come from the authenticated files or records of agencies that can confirm what you say. Testimony is another word for witness. If you witnessed an experience of which you speak, then you were there as it happened. Witnesses, also called eyewitnesses, frequently have the best kind of proof possible.

There is much to know about proving what you say. Many kinds of language need to be avoided because they lessen one's credibility. The foremost of these is equivocation, use of the same word or phrase for two different things. For example, the word "bad" has come to mean both "bad" and "good." In the sentence "He plays a bad horn," bad means good. If you say "He's a bad person," you mean bad in the sense of evil, the opposite of good. The word "boss" has also come to mean more than one thing. "Boss," in the traditional sense, connotes the person you work for, whereas "boss" in the current slang sense means very good. The sentence "This is a boss restaurant" means that it is a cut above the rest.

Ambiguous talk is another kind of language that reduces your chances of being believed. This kind of speech has to do with sentences that are unclear as they are spoken. The slogan "Save soap and waste paper" can be interpreted in two ways. You can read "Save soap and save waste paper," or you can read "Save soap and throw away paper." Either way you hear it, the original phrase is open to question. If you look at the language of wills, you can see why the courts have such difficulty with bequests. The statement, "I give and bequeath the amount of $25,000 to my wife and my son John," can be interpreted in two ways:

I give and bequeath the amount of $25,000 to my wife and $25,000 to my son John, or,
I give and bequeath the amount of $12,500 to my wife and $12,500 to my son John.

When lawyers, politicians, and professors talk in ambiguous language, they say things like "I believe in the equalization of the tax laws, or revenue distribution." This sentence can also mean two things. The connective word "or" is critical. You can substitute "and" for "or," or you can substitute "which is" for "or." Either substitution changes the meaning radically.

If you use vague or fuzzy terminology, your credibility is lessened even more. Vague expressions need clarification by definition. Whenever you use an abstract noun in speech, you are in danger of being vague and therefore not understood. Such nouns include words you use everyday without thinking: friendship, peace, honor, stability, trust, hope, love, brilliance. All of the emotional words have vague definitions because they mean something different to every speaker and hearer. When you glibly toss off the word "peace," do you mean that "peace" is the absence of war, or that it is the absence of internal conflicts? Whatever you do mean by "peace," you should be ready to define it. Without definition we all walk in different worlds. There is a passage in the novel *Madame Bovary* by Gustav Flaubert in which the suicidal heroine Emma Bovary says to her detractors something to the effect that "if you wish to converse with me, define your terms." This is fine advice, because it reduces the use of unclear words. If "honor" means, to you, not getting caught, it might mean to someone else "going a step beyond what is expected," and to a third person "giving your life for a friend." These definitions are drastically different in concept and execution. Say which one you mean if you want to be believed. It would be well to rethink your own values for words, rather than to leave them foggy. Ask yourself what you really mean by the term "friend." Is a friend one who would lay down his life for you, or someone from whom you can freely borrow a cup of sugar? Words can run the gamut of emotional meaning. "Love," for instance, is a word that has been widely bandied about. If by "love" you mean "like," or "care for," be sure to say so. Consider the vocabularies associated with the word "love." We say "falling in love." Why not "rising in love," because love is such a positive, hopeful emotion? "Heart" is another example of a word with various meanings. When you say that someone "has a good heart," you usually mean that he or she is generous, outgoing, giving, sharing. "A good heart" can also describe a physical organ that functions at peak form. Be sure to put a price tag on the emotional meanings you give to words. Weigh these meanings according to your conscience.

When you use emotionally loaded language, you give yourself away. We tend to hang on to what is currently aired around town. "Chauvinist" continues to describe "sexist" or "racist" attitudes, but it is used loosely to mean a host of unfavorable personal qualities. Police officers have been labeled "pigs" by those who interpret police stories in an

unfavorable light. For many years intellectually slow children have been labeled "dummies" or "retards." Others with more understanding of and sympathy for their condition have created a new category: the exceptional child. When you think about it, all children, bright or slow, are exceptional. Slower children are exceptional in a way different from bright ones. They perceive unusual detail in a way that escapes "quicker" children. They tend to remember people's names more readily, especially those who care about them. They frequently recall a color, size, or shape that has caught their eye, even in an out-of-the-way place. In short, they are "exceptional" in affection and devotion, whereas other "brighter" children are exceptional in attention and concentration.

There are still other ways in which your words can belie your credibility. One of these ways is through the continual use of overstatement, or exaggeration. Why do most of us feel that holding to fact is a less imaginative way of speech? Consider all the stories you hear about your friends' adventures and mishaps. How many of these stories are fact? How many are fact-plus-embellishment? Fantasy does enter into the world of verbal expression, as with the proverbial fisherman's story of "the one that got away." If the fisherman reported to his friends only the fish he actually had in his catch, would his friends like him less? No. But our need to be exceptional at times is a common reason for boasting. Exaggerated talk offers us the chance to shine at the center of the group, but it has the cumulative impact of reducing our credibility. After a while, if you can't "tell it like it is," your gift for exaggeration will be the least appreciated of all your talents.

Your credibility can also be determined by how you talk about others. If you are known as one who continually undermines the character of another, your own reputation will suffer as a consequence. Such is the case with gossips, who tell all they hear—and more—to anyone who will lend an ear. Gossips always have an audience, because we are always interested in the way others lead their lives. But the gossip has a poor credit rating of his own. People in his presence will wonder what will be said of them after they leave. Attacking the character or competence of another assures that someone, in return, will attack ours. The successful talker knows the high price of mediocrity in speech. He steers clear of people-talk and concentrates mostly on idea-talk and event-talk.

We can attack another's character by assuming that if a person has a weakness in one area of his life, it will spread to the rest of his life like wildfire. You hear people say, "Don't bother with Ed. He left his wife and children. He must be impossible to live with." Although Ed may not have been a good husband and father, he may thoroughly engage himself in his work. People may find him a compatible work partner. Failing in one of life's commitments does not mean that one is a washout in others. Another example of extended judgments occurs when we assume that success in one facet of life breeds success in all facets. We hear remarks like "Roy is such a good husband and father.

He'd have my vote if he ran for county sheriff." Is it reasonable to assume that because a person does well in his home life, he would do well as a public servant? We would be more credible in our judgment if we said that Roy would make a fine sheriff because he did well in sheriff school.

Another proof of your personal credibility lies in the area of consistency. Consistency of character implies that you think through what you want to believe in and hold to it with steadfast conviction. Some people are difficult to believe because they change their minds on important issues from day to day. What is truly vital to your life shouldn't be changed. What is incidental can be changed, and often is, with each day. For example, if you believe that most people you come in contact with are fundamentally honest, hard-working, and easy to communicate with, your life will reflect that judgment. It is a major part of your philosophy. A minor reflection of that philosophy might show itself in how you reveal your trusting nature. You might lend small amounts of cash to people because you believe that they will pay you back. Inner consistency has to do with solid, unchanging values. If one of the people to whom you lend money never pays you back, it is a minor consideration to you. Still strong is your consistent belief that people are honest. Most of your acquaintances continue to bear out your reasoning. Being consistent with yourself simply means being true to the script you have written for yourself. You are not swayed easily, but you are open to change when change is necessary to reconfirm your beliefs.

Reduction of your credibility occurs when you are too emotional or hotheaded about issues and answers. If you are known to fly off the handle with your words and actions, you won't be among the first to be consulted in matters of importance. Ways of showing too much emotional language can be detected in the following areas:

Appeal to pity. This is the dialogue of the downtrodden: "Look how hard I work and slave to keep all of you together. Poor me. Nobody would care if I died tomorrow." On another level, appeals to pity come at us with every magazine we read. A caption reads: "You can help us, or you can turn the page." Everyone who turns the page finds himself feeling guilty that he didn't help. Yet the reader could himself be in need of help to keep his own little family together.

Appeal to fear. This kind of credibility-shaker takes the verbal form of "I told you that this would happen if . . ." An example of fear-appeal occurred a few years ago during the national threat of a swine-flu epidemic. We were told that if we neglected to be inoculated we would all surely perish. Most people rejected the vaccine and avoided the flu anyway. When we make fear-appeals too strong, we acquire a reputation for overstating, that is, exaggerating the scope of a crisis before the crisis arrives.

Appeal to authority. We weaken our believability when we assume that because a person is an authority in one specialized area, he is equally capable in other areas. For example, General George Patton was a famous military strategist of World War II. His opinions on military matters were respected and sought after. Yet after the war his usefulness was outlived, and he was seldom consulted on matters of national import. This is the natural ebb and flow of the human resourcefulness chart. We spend our whole lives learning about some small area in this vast planet to which we'd like to devote our most productive hours. If we know one thing well, that is usually enough for a lifetime. We can always spend any extra time learning a little about a lot of lesser things. When we appeal to authority in our talk, we must remember to know the limitations of that authority. We can eagerly consult Dr. Spock on matters pertaining to the growth and development of infants. We'd never think of consulting him about a real estate purchase or a national election campaign. When you quote authorities on any subject, be sure to remember their names and their qualifications. It lowers your verbal credit rating when you say "An authority on this subject says . . ." Tell which authority and list his record of achievements.

Appeal to tradition. You can know much about how a person thinks by the way he is rooted in custom. Some people are used to certain ways of doing things and are not anxious to learn new approaches. When an employer says to a worker:

> That's a good idea you've come up with, but we've done it this way for twenty years. What you propose to do just isn't done,

his words reveal that his preferences are rooted in the past and are not likely to change. The words you speak tell more about you than the clothes you wear and the home you live in. A simple sentence like the one above reveals an entire philosophy of operation.

Additional dangers to your credibility set in whenever you use technical language in talk. Technical language implies the use of long, unfamiliar words, assuming a certain level of understanding among the listeners. Be not impressed by a speaker who indulges in many-syllabled words in the hope of demonstrating his extensive knowledge. Appealing to your hearers' ignorance turns them away from your style and content. If you can't say your ideas in simple terms, you probably can't say your ideas at all. To look upon your audience as inferior is to alienate them entirely. Once a talker intimates to his hearers:

> Listen, this is really difficult stuff. You probably will find it impossible to grasp, but I'll try to find words that your limited resources can absorb . . . ,

he has lost them forever.

Another kind of talk to avoid if we are interested in our credibility is trivial. People can go around a circle of trivia without ever stating their main message. Trivia, or small talk, can bog you down so that you wonder what you started out to say. Trivia is like cheap jewelry. You can see it, but it in no way beautifies the wearer. The absence of it would help you to concentrate on the person and the message.

The above messages have to do with proving yourself as a respected, successful talker. To persuade others to see your possibilities and know your worth is the chief reason for talk. We have listed several ideas to help you to reduce the level of nonbelief in your words. Remember, people believe you at first because they have no reason not to. Once you have gained a foothold on respectability in the art of talk and can exchange your views frankly and unaffectedly, you are well on the road to a bright future.

In Style

You have a special style, that is, a way of captivating others, that is unique to you. In its broadest sense, style is the manner in which you choose to express yourself. It is the means at your disposal of persuading others to be attentive to your abilities. Whatever style is natural and comfortable for you should be your trademark. As an expression of your personality, style implies a degree of professional polish. Whether you tend to be a quiet observer, a whimsical philosopher, or a life-of-the-party type, trust yourself to *be* yourself.

Whatever mannerisms your special style includes, when you persuade others to believe in you, you need to be aware of the process involved in it. Steps in persuasive talk include the development of style through the following procedures:

Getting attention. When you engage in talk that is supposed to sell you to success, you must find ways of securing and holding the attention of your listeners. If you have only one listener, as in an important conversation, this procedure is no less important. Notice how a young man about to propose marriage to his girlfriend will take great care to set the scene. He'll reserve a special table with candlelight in a fine restaurant to make sure that his girlfriend is in the right atmosphere to listen. He needs all the attention he can get to improve his chances for an affirmative response.

Talk is persuasion in action. When you talk to more than one person, you still need to fix their attention on what you are about to say. If your audience is allowed to wander mentally *before* you begin to speak, they will never be fully yours. Consider the style of the late comedian Jack Benny. In one of his later radio broadcasts, a thief demanded from the great "cheapskate," "Your money or your life." A very long silence was Benny's response. No need for words. The audience's laughter was longer than the silence. Benny had his listeners riveted to him from the start. However many people comprise your audience, you must secure their attention *before* you speak, as soon as your physical self appears. Think of new and fresh ways of beginning your words. If you fall back on "I'd just like to say a few words about . . . ," you risk a mental exodus of your audience.

Once a student of political history, who was interested in the state of the economy, spoke to a group of associates about the impact of inflation on their lives. The subject of inflation can be a bore because we think that everything that can be said about it has been said. "Oh, *that* again," is the anticipated response. The student knew that his credibility would be enhanced if he came up with something original about inflation in order to gain the attention of his audience. He did just that. When he took his stand at the podium, he reached deep into his pockets and threw two handfuls of pennies into the audience. The pennies rolled along the floor after they showered the room. The student's opening remark followed immediately. He said that he was throwing away his pennies because they had become worthless due to inflation. He wouldn't miss the small impact of their buying power. His message was received by willing ears because it was offered in a new key, a different style.

Holding attention. To hold the attention of your listeners you need to have access to a whole range of devices. If you intend to interact with them during your discussion, you can use ready-made phrases that prod others to think out loud and respond to your ideas. These phrases include:

a. "Of course, you're familiar with . . ." This remark leaves the audience free to say that they are or aren't familiar with your message content. Sometimes people say that they *are* familiar with what you are saying because they think everyone around them knows something they don't know.

b. "Can I assume then . . . ?" This prod allows your hearers to open up the contents of their minds. The phrase usually provides for much stimulating dialogue between talker and listeners.

c. "What would be your reaction to . . . ?" This question is another design for encouraging the easy flow of words among talker and participants. It helps to maintain audience interest when you invite them to "co-host" with you.

Maintaining interest can be done in other ways. You can justify the reason for your talk by telling the audience what's in it for them. For example, if you have broken the habit of chain-smoking and you want to tell others how you did it, be sure to announce yourself as a former six-pack-a-day smoker. Your credibility would be boosted by this bond with the audience. It would be foolish indeed to stand before people who are trying to quit smoking and announce that you sympathize with their problem but you have never smoked cigarettes. The establishment of a common ground is the key to successful talk.

You hold people's attention when you keep reminding yourself to narrow your topic to a certain *facet* of a problem or issue. Most of us attempt to talk on subjects that are clearly too broad in scope. The audience gets lost in the shuffle of too many thoughts and ideas. If your subject is inflation, you can't, in five or ten minutes, give the history of inflation, the causes of inflation, and the prospects for the future. Such an overwhelming task is the object of many books. In five or ten minutes, you would fare better if you narrowed your topic to one aspect of inflation, like "The Fall of the Penny."

Attention is also maintained by presenting your qualifications to talk. People like to know who you are and how you came to know what you speak of. Personal data is an appealing audience holder.

Audiences need to have terms defined as they first appear in your talk. If you speak of vague concepts such as "maximum efficiency" or "solar bankruptcy," say precisely what you mean by each of these phrases. Listeners fail to follow talkers who lead them down many paths to confusion and bewilderment. If each word you choose means all that it can and should mean, you will have little to worry about as a skilled talker.

Producing the desired response. Structure or aim your words at a specific conclusion. If you are talking at a job interview, the desired response is that you are hired. If your intention in talking is to get a few people to donate a pint of blood to the local hospital, appeal to their head and heart, that is, to their intellect and emotions, in a way they cannot refuse. And by all means, have the bloodmobile handy, just outside the door. When you persuade people to do difficult things, such as giving their time or money to a specific cause, you are in fact doing double work as a persuader. You first have to persuade them to believe in your cause; then you have to *move* them to action. The "action" part is the most challenging. Be sure that you stay to see the action through, if action is your intention. For example, if you have persuaded your hearers to write to their congressman about a particular social issue, don't let your argument rest until you have seen it through to the end. Supply the paper, pen, envelope, stamp, and name and address of the congressman. Then give them time to write the letter while you are all together. If you send an audience away to do "homework," they won't. See your project through while your inspiration is still with the group. The effect of your persuasive hold over them diminishes very rapidly after you stop talking.

Style is all-important when it comes to the injection of humor into your words. The safest advice about humor is to avoid it unless you were born into the special world of the comic and intend to make a living from your wit. If you ever make your listeners laugh, it probably will be by accident. When you plan a funny thing to say, it usually falls flat. Humor is spontaneous, of the moment. It can never be anticipated or duplicated.

The last consideration of style here is the forceful, belligerent manner versus the humble or conciliatory one. Both extremes should be avoided; the first, for being too strong and overbearing, the second, for being weak and apologetic. A forceful talker may give the audience the impression that he is saying to himself, "What do they know?" He may be a shy person who has forced himself to overcompensate and has gone too far. Such a person usually has to have the floor constantly and doesn't risk interaction with his listeners. For all his force and flourish, he is fearful of failure and doesn't know how to control his fear. The meek talker, on the other hand, doesn't inherit the earth or his audience. Being too humble in style conveys the message: "Hello. I'm sorry." Try to find the middle lane, and work your style around it. Middle-lane talkers know that they are never as fully prepared as they could be, but they have practiced and prepared as much as possible in the time available to them. They feel that they have a pretty good handle on their subject, they are willing to share what they know with others, and they are willing to exchange ideas freely and openly. They don't mind being questioned on their subject, and they can accept being in the wrong occasionally. They are, in a word, "together" with themselves in a living and learning experience.

Ask Me

When the writer Gertrude Stein lay dying, her friends gathered around her bedside hoping to hear from her the wisdom of all her years. They begged her to say something. They kept asking her, "What's the answer?" She, with a confident little smile, responded after a time, "What's the question?" Whenever we talk, we have a chance to use the old reliable Socratic method of dialogue: the question and answer. It tells others how we think and feel. It answers questions that we have of others. The successful talker knows how to field questions and give answers. He knows that the most valuable reply of all may be, "I don't know the answer to that question. I'd be happy to look it up and let you know the next time we meet." Not knowing all the answers confirms us as members in good standing of the human race. It also endears us to our listeners much more than a circular answer that seems evasive. Here are some ways of dealing with question-and-answer talk in the best possible style.

1. If the person asking the question can't be heard by others, repeat the question from where you are. Then answer it.

2. Answer questions as quickly and as simply as you can. Don't go into an overlong, complicated statement that is more inclusive than your talk in total. If a question can be answered thoroughly enough in a few words, be grateful.

3. Include every one of your listeners when taking questions from the floor. See if you can get a representation of questions from all corners of the room. If you are fielding questions from a long table of seated guests, be sure that you pick up as many questions on the right as you do on the left side of the table.

4. If two people ask the same question and you have answered it once to the audience's satisfaction, it means that the second questioner was "tuned out" when the question was asked the first time. Be gracious enough to answer it again, simply and directly. Don't say "Weren't you listening? I just answered that."

5. Anticipate two or three main questions that might be asked, and prepare those answers in advance. Then they will not make you uneasy or throw you off when they arise.

6. While you are being asked a question, fix your eyes on the person asking it. In this way he knows you care about what he says. Don't do anything that might distract you from him. Stand or sit perfectly

still; try not to cough, sneeze, clean your glasses, or recross your legs while the questioner speaks. The successful talker is also a successful listener.

7. Be sure to hold questioners to their questions. Don't encourage them to go beyond the scope of the question by giving their advice or opinions.

8. Don't extend the question–answer session beyond the allotted time. Always state what the time is. Say, for example, that there will be a twenty-minute interval for questions. Don't exceed that period.

How Well Am I Doing?

Mayor Edward Koch of New York City is frequently televised as he asks his constituents for their appraisal of his administrative work. "How am I doing?" he inquires. That, of course, is another way of saying, "Do you like me? Are you glad you voted for me?" As you talk your way to success, you want to know how you are doing from time to time. Here is a checklist of points to consider as your talk becomes more polished and professional.

1. Are you honest and fair to yourself and your listeners? Don't exceed your margin of competency by talking about things you don't know well.

2. Do you really care about communicating well with people? Does your body go through the motions of talk but the spirit lag behind in some other time and space?

3. Do you mind being in the wrong at times? Remember, everyone is in the wrong many times each day. The trick is to accept it as a way of life and growth. You can always try to be less wrong but know that you can never be *all* right.

4. Do you ask questions when you have them? Timid people seldom get the chance to have their questions clarified and go away knowing no more than when they came. Every question, even the most complicated, deserves some kind of answer.

5. Do you stick to your point? Be sure to defend your own opinions, once you have studied and prepared them. Others will respect you

more for not shifting ground to conform to what the majority wants.

6. Is there evidence that you study the characteristics of your audience? Good talk can be spoken on many levels. To know the level of your audience each time you talk is a tremendous boost to your credibility.

7. Do you speak loud enough to be heard? If you don't, go back to the breathing exercises in Chapter III and practice volume control.

8. What is the total impression made by your words? The ideal impression is to leave your listeners wanting more. They will remember your name and your impact and want to hear you again. If you expect to talk with a group only once, you know that the impact is lasting. If you intend to be with one group frequently, that is, two or three times a week, you had better leave them wanting more each time you conclude. Such a feeling maintains enthusiasm for your style and content and is a good ego-builder.

9. Are your ideas well-organized? Be sure to go from A to B, rather than from M to T. Listeners find any kind of disorder a major distraction.

10. Do you make adjustments easily to accommodate the noise factor in talk? Any kind of stimulus apart from your words will disturb your communication. Wait until obvious noise subsides before you continue.

11. Do you feel that you are a valuable asset to any group or person who listens to you? How you feel about yourself is communicated instantly by the way you walk and stand, by the way you pick things up and hold them in your hand. To have a good feeling about yourself is to believe that, without you, the person or group would function less effectively.

12. Are you always aware of the importance of eye-touch, and other kinds of body-talk? Look for signals in your audience that tell you how well you are doing.

13. Do you know when to stop? A good rule of thumb is to stop while you are doing well. When your listeners are in the palm of your hand and your message has reached them in the way you intended, stop. To say any more would be to undo the impact. The expression "Quit while you're ahead" has merit when it comes to talking.

14. Does your mind wander when others speak to you? Are you

suddenly caught off-guard when someone asks you for a response to their remarks and you haven't "heard" a thing? Practice the art of listening. It will add a measure of grace to your own success as a talker.

Talking is a practical matter. Talking well is an art. It is of vital importance to your private and professional dreams. To talk with clarity is a gift. To talk with confidence is an absolute trust.

Man's mind stretched to a new idea never goes back to its original dimensions.

—Oliver Wendell Holmes

Selected Bibliography

Andersen, Martin P., Lewis, Wesley, and Murray, James. *The Speaker and His Audience.* New York: Harper and Row, Publishers, 1964.

Banville, Thomas G. *How to Listen—How to Be Heard.* Chicago: Nelson-Hall, Inc., 1978.

Berlo, David K. *The Process of Communication.* New York: Holt, Rinehart and Winston, 1960.

Davitz, Joel R., ed. *The Communication of Emotional Meaning.* New York: McGraw-Hill Book Company, 1964.

Ellingsworth, Huber W., and Clevenger, Theodore, Jr. *Speech and Social Action.* Englewood Cliffs, New Jersey: Prentice-Hall, 1967.

Fast, Julius. *Body Language.* New York: M. Evans and Company, 1970.

Howard, Jane. *Please Touch.* New York: McGraw-Hill Book Company, 1970.

Keltner, John. *Interpersonal Speech Communication.* Belmont, California: Wadsworth Publishing Company, 1970.

Mills, Glen E. *Message Preparation: Analysis and Structure.* New York: Bobbs-Merrill Company, 1966.

Montagu, Ashley. *Learning Non-Aggression.* New York: Oxford University Press, 1978.

Scheidel, Thomas M. *Persuasive Speaking.* Glenview, Illinois: Scott, Foresman and Company, 1967.

Whyte, William H. *Is Anybody Listening?* New York: Simon and Schuster, 1952.